101 Best Ways
to Be Your Best

*101 Stories, Essays and Ideas to
Help You Operate at Your Personal
and Professional Best*

Michael Angier

SUCCESS NETWORKS INTERNATIONAL

Published by
Success Networks International, Inc.
Win-Win Way, PO Box 2048
South Burlington, Vermont 05407-2048
www.SuccessNet.org

Other *101 Best Ways* books and booklets available at www.101BestWays.com

- ☑ 101 Best Ways to Get Ahead

- ☑ 101 Best Ways to Simplify Your Life – coming in late 2005

- ☑ 101 Best Ways to Stay Motivated – coming in 2006

Limit of Liability/Disclaimer of Warranty
While the author has used his best efforts in preparing this book, he makes no representation or warranties with respect to the accuracy or completeness of the contents and specifically disclaims any implied warranties. You should consult with a professional where appropriate. The author and publishers shall not be liable for any loss of profit or any other commercial damages, including but not limited to special, incidental, consequential or other damages.

Library of Congress Cataloging-in-Publication Data

Angier, Michael E.

101 Best Ways to Be Your Best : 101 Stories, Essays and Ideas to Help You Operate at Your Personal and Professional Best / Michael E. Angier.—1st ed.

p. cm.
Includes index.
ISBN 0-9704175-4-3

1. Success . 2. Self-Development. I. Angier, Michael E. II. Title: 101 Best Ways to Be Your Best III. Title.

2005903600

Praise for *101 Best Ways to Be Your Best*

"I've always thought Michael Angier was one of the very best web-based personal development authors. His new book proves once again he clearly understands and communicates the keys to maximizing personal performance. Buy it. Use it. Live it."

—Vic Johnson
founder, www.AsAManThinketh.net

"Michael Angier has done it again. Here are more helpful tools to keep you motivated and sharp in your quest for your dream. From dealing with overwhelm to suggesting ways to stay inspired, it's as if he can see inside our heads and anticipate all our possible dream roadblocks. Thanks, Michael! We needed this!"

—Suzanne Falter-Barns
author of *Living Your Joy*
www.GetKnownNow.com

"In the personal development field today, Michael Angier is a national treasure. In our fast-paced and often confusing world, we need leaders more than ever—leaders with integrity, with vision and most importantly, the ability to touch our hearts and help us see a brighter future for ourselves. This book is a gem. Read it, use it and pass it on."

—Sterling Valentine
www.SterlingValentine.com

"When one thinks of success these days, the name of Michael Angier usually comes to mind. Do yourself and your business or career a great favor and get a copy of Michael's new offering, 101 Best Ways to Be Your Best *and begin to benefit from the wisdom and great advice of this stellar entrepreneur!"*

—Rick Beneteau
www.BetterSalesRightNow.com

101 Best Ways to Be Your Best

"101 Best Ways to Be Your Best *is an incredible resource. If you have serious plans and goals to be the best in whatever you do, then consider this book indispensable. My advice—get it, read it, follow it!*"

—Randy Gilbert
host of *The Inside Success Show*
bestseller mentor www.BestSellerU.com

"*Each piece brims with insight and wisdom . . . Worth gold!*"

—Joe Vitale
author of *The Attractor Factor*
www.MrFire.com

"*Michael Angier gives a textbook full of the ABC's to success. A must read—and a very enjoyable one as well!*"

—Jim Rohn
author of *The Five Major Pieces to the Life Puzzle*
and America's Foremost Business Philosopher
www.JimRohn.com

"*Michael wants to help you operate at your personal and professional best. I learn a lot from him. You can, too.*"

—Burt Dubin
Personal Achievement Institute
www.SpeakingBizSuccess.com

"*If you're looking for simple ways to inspire the dreamer within you and make your vision real, Michael Angier's new* 101 Best Ways to Be Your Best *will be the catalyst that will launch your impossible dreams into reality.*"

—Paul Bauer
author of *Dream-Minder* and *Creating Abundance*
www.DreamsAlive.com

"*Michael has woven a masterful tapestry of ageless wisdom and life lessons. This book provides a real soul enriching experience you'll savor.*"

—Kristie Tamsevicius
bestselling author, business speaker and consultant
www.KristieT.com

"101 Best Ways to Be Your Best *is one of those rare gems that comes along once in a great while. Brief and extremely practical, but based on timeless truths, this is a book to keep nearby for ready reference, or by the coffee pot so you start each morning filled with inspiration and reminded of your highest aspirations. Michael has collected the 'best of the best' and put it in a handy format that I will read and re-read for years to come. Highly recommended!"*

—Philip E. Humbert, PhD
author, speaker and coach
www.PhilipHumbert.com

"Your journey to success will definitely be accelerated by reading Michael Angier's timely, practical and motivating book, 101 Ways to Be Your Best. *With years of experience to back up every word, Michael points out the fast track and supports you to run to your dreams. Read this book, subscribe to his newsletter and buy his materials. Get as much 'Michael Angier' as you possibly can . . . if success is important to you."*

—Rhoberta Shaler, PhD
author of *Wrestling Rhinos:
Conquering Conflict in the Wilds of Work*
www.OptimizeInstitute.com

"Michael Angier is one of those very special people who have carved their way through life's challenges and come out on top positive, optimistic and caring. His writings share the best of his well-earned wisdom and always uplift and inspire. And, I might add, he has finely polished writing skills that bring it all home with humor, finesse and panache. I highly recommend Michael's great new book is for anyone looking for an immediate—and enduring—motivational and inspirational boost."

—Dr. Jill Ammon-Wexler
author of *Take Charge: 14 Steps to Smash Your Limits*
www.Quantum-Self.com

Table of Contents

Acknowledgements

No book is the result of one person's efforts.

First I would like to thank the members and subscribers of SuccessNet. Most of the chapters were written for them over the course of several years. Without their patronage and support, I would not have had the wealth of material *101 Best Ways to Be Your Best* contains.

They offered much appreciated feedback and encouragement. Their belief that I have something worthwhile to offer made the whole project doable.

I am blessed with a beautiful and loving partner in life. My wife Dawn is my friend, my confidant, my teacher and my business partner. She not only has supported and encouraged my writing, she's worked diligently to proof, edit and correct my work. When I met and fell in love with her, I had no idea she was such a talented copy editor. She makes me look good.

Several friends and colleagues reviewed this book, offered tips and provided dependable and objective perspectives, which enhanced the value of every page. I am grateful.

My Master Mind Group has always been there for me. Our weekly meetings have provided ideas, encouragement, objectivity, focus and inspiration. Thank you.

Sarah Pond, our Creative Maximizer and Membership Director has provided me with invaluable support. I don't know what I would do without her.

My family has put up with my being absorbed and often unavailable as I wrote articles and chapters on deadline. I appreciate their patience.

Last and certainly not least, I thank God for the many blessings that have been bestowed upon me. I'm exceptionally grateful I was born into the greatest country in the world at the greatest time in history with talents and resources only Universal Intelligence could have created.

My thanks to all who contribute to my life and my work.

Foreword by JoAnna Brandi

I have this strange relationship with books. When it's time for me to learn something new, the book I need will somehow find me. It may fall off a shelf at my feet or nudge itself a little further out of the book rack to catch my attention or vibrate with an energy that makes it "glow." No matter, when a book wants my attention, it shows up at my door. I've learned that I'd best read that book to receive the gift of another piece to the puzzle I call my life.

This book has just shown up at your door. Welcome it in like an old friend. Put on a pot of tea or grab a soda, relax and explore what this book holds for you.

There's something here you wanted. There's something here that answers a question you didn't know you had. There's a story, a passage, a quote that will lift your spirits, touch your heart and give you support on a day when you're feeling the need.

I'm honored to be the official "greeter." Welcome to Michael Angier's world! It's a positive place filled with commitment, adventure, strength, challenge, insight, common sense, opportunity and wisdom.

I can't tell you exactly how long I've known Michael, but I know it's been many years. I can't even tell you how Michael found his way into my life, but I know it had something to do with the magic of the Internet and my strong belief that when a student is ready the teacher appears.

And appears and appears and appears. Michael's wisdom shows up on my desktop every week. I visit his world often, and now you can, too. Through the years I've known him, his words have challenged me, needled me, inspired me, soothed me, made me laugh and brought me to tears. He has often reminded me of my responsibilities as a leader, assured me there's no such thing as failure and modeled a way of being I admire. His "right on the money" advice is grounded and real. His skill in combining a story that resonates with a "to-do" that motivates will get you moving in a positive direction.

Michael and I are kindred spirits, both crazy enough to think we can change the world with our work, both with a bias towards action and a decidedly optimistic view of the world. As you read this book and come to treasure the stories, as I have, you'll find yourself thinking differently. You'll ask yourself more interesting and more provocative questions. You'll get some new and more productive answers. If you follow his suggestions, you'll find yourself more positive, more powerful and more prosperous. And I'm willing to bet you'll receive a few pieces to the puzzle of your life.

Michael calls himself the CIO of his company—the Chief Inspiration Officer. You'll see how well he does his job as you read this book. It's a collection of his best stories. I'm thrilled, as you'll be, to see those stories, all in one place, ready to inspire you just when you need it.

So come on, dig in! Start from the beginning or do what I do—close your eyes, hold the book in your hands, get very still and let your intuition lead you to the perfect page, the perfect message, the perfect answer to the question you didn't know you had.

—JoAnna Brandi
author of *54 Ways to Stay Positive in a Changing, Challenging and Sometimes Negative World* and *Building Customer Loyalty—21 Essential Elements in ACTION*
www.CustomerCareCoach.com

Introduction

For the past few years, the default email address for my company has been *BeYourBest@SuccessNet.org*. It seemed appropriate, since that's what we're dedicated to doing—helping people be their best—personally and professionally.

And it's that mission that has directed the writing of each of the following 101 chapters. This book is a compilation of the most popular articles I've written for my members and subscribers since 1996. Each of them is intended to help you achieve your full and unique potential.

You could say it took over ten years to write this book. And when you consider I drew from over three decades of research and experience, you might say it took even longer.

Why You Should Read this Book

101 Best Ways to Be Your Best offers a collection of short, simple, insightful concepts that have been proven to work and *will* work in your life. It's practical wisdom from my particular point of view.

Some chapters will remind you of something you already know. Others will introduce new ideas you can use to accomplish more and experience less frustration. They're all designed to help you make your life work better.

As you read, you'll find these proven principles of success and achievement sinking into your consciousness and positively impacting your life and the lives of those around you.

How You Should Read 101 Best Ways to Be Your Best

This book does not need to be read in any logical order. Start wherever you like. Open the book to any chapter. And when you reread a chapter at another time or place, you'll likely find it saying something different to you.

Don't allow the simplicity of these concepts to take away from their power. Sift through these pages with an open mind and let the stories do their work. Take the best and leave the rest.

Success is fun. Have fun with it.

Icons in this Book

As you read this book, you'll notice special graphics. These are icons to help emphasize action points and resources.

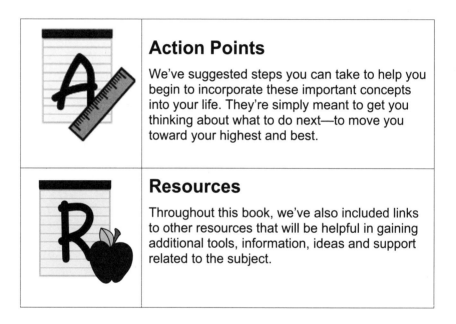

Action Points

We've suggested steps you can take to help you begin to incorporate these important concepts into your life. They're simply meant to get you thinking about what to do next—to move you toward your highest and best.

Resources

Throughout this book, we've also included links to other resources that will be helpful in gaining additional tools, information, ideas and support related to the subject.

1. Live the Dream

I've always been fascinated by dreamers. And making dreams come true for myself and others is what my life is about.

When I was in my teens, I started to think seriously about where I wanted my life to go. Like many young people, I had visions of doing something significant. I also knew that most people abandon their dreams. So I promised myself that I would never give up trying, no matter what difficulties might come.

And the difficult times did come—some of them more painful than I could have imagined. But I kept my promise. I've never given up. I've been blown out of the sky several times, but I've always been able to put things back together and lumber down the runway to bluer skies.

My greatest fear had always been that I might reach the end of my life and feel I hadn't fulfilled my purpose—that I hadn't made a lasting difference in the world. I no longer have this fear, although I'm still driven to make the most of my talents, my experiences and my resources.

During my 30-plus years of personal development research, I've seen many people—good people, hard-working people, talented people— fail to experience the success they deserved.

They weren't actually failing, they were just no longer willing to go for the best that's within them. They had good intentions, but somewhere along the line they got disheartened and gave up on themselves—they let their dreams slip away.

It was out of my commitment and this concern, as well as my own failings, that I started SuccessNet. What I try to do with my writing and with this network is to coach people to be their best—personally and professionally. No professional athlete would consider competing without a coach. And yet, few people have a coach for the game of life. Coaches challenge and motivate the player. A good coach will help the athlete develop a game plan and create accountability for following that plan.

And we all need a game plan—a plan for a balanced, value-driven, principle-centered life. I believe that happiness is a result of continually striving toward worthwhile objectives while also enjoying and appreciating what is here and now. It's a paradoxical balance struck between what I call "inspirational dissatisfaction" and contentment.

By investing the time and energy to get clear on our values and life purpose, by defining and articulating what we really want from all areas of our life, and then consistently acting on our objectives, we will live a successful life. This kind of work isn't easy. It requires deep thinking and honest soul-searching. It's not something you do in an afternoon. It demands constant focus and attention. Unless you're the architect of your life, you're at the effect of everything and everyone you encounter. It's something with which we all need help.

My passion is helping people discover, develop and fulfill their dreams. In the process, I fulfill my own. I take great joy in supporting people and organizations to consistently create excellence. To participate in the development and realization of a dream is, for me, to walk upon holy ground. By living our dreams, we give birth to things that never would have been, but more importantly, we become more of who we are in the process.

"There is only one success—to be able to spend your life in your own way."

—Christopher Morley

"The best reason for having dreams is that in dreams no reasons are necessary."

—Ashleigh Brilliant

"I've dreamt in my life dreams that have stayed with me ever after, and changed my ideas; they've gone through and through me, like wine through water, and altered the color of my mind."

—Emily Bronte

"You see things and you say 'Why?'. But I dream things that never were, and I say 'Why Not?'"

—George Bernard Shaw

2. Clarity of Purpose

Living a Rich Life

If becoming rich is part of your dream—and there's no reason why it shouldn't be—just be careful you don't confuse being rich with living a rich life. I think we should all become financially rich. If we are, we can give more to our families, our communities and our world. But it's living a rich life that should be our primary objective.

A rich life is created by being more concerned with who you become than what you acquire. It's created by clarity of purpose. And clarity leads to power.

In my opinion, the most important thing you can do for yourself is to invest the time and perhaps even money to become absolutely clear on what you want out of life. I'm not talking about goals here. I'm talking about the essence of what you truly want—what you will feel good about when your life is over. This is not an easy process. Perhaps that's why so few people do it.

All the information is inside you. You need only to think carefully and intuit deeply in order to gain this insight and allow yourself to live with a keen focus and real clarity.

The old adage, "Know thyself," has become such a cliché that it's lost much of its meaning. But when you're completely clear on who you are, what you want, where you're going and have a plan to get there, you'll not only be more effective, you'll experience better health and more fulfillment. You will lead a rich life.

If we were sitting across from one another, here's what I'd ask you: "What's the most important goal/dream/mission in your life?"

I would look for a description that shows your passion for it—something where you have a sparkle in your eye and emotion in your voice. I believe that everyone has a dream—that it's not something to be invented, but rather to be discovered. It may take some time to uncover it, but living a life filled with verve and excitement is certainly worth it.

Your plan, your vehicle to get there may change over time, but the vision—the mission—will not.

The next question I would ask is, "Why do you want to accomplish this dream?" Your reasons are critical to your success. When you have sufficient reasons, you can overcome any challenge. One way you can strengthen your reasons is to visualize what your life will be like when you've accomplished your dream. The more real it becomes—the more you see it and feel it—the more you'll believe it.

It's also a way to check out if this is really *your* dream. Sometimes, after envisioning what we think is our dream, we find that it's not really what we want. Better to find out now than to spend our lives achieving something that will not provide fulfillment in the process.

And it is that process that is the real value. Remember, it's not so much what you accomplish, but rather what you become in that process that's important. Which leads me to my next question.

"How will you have to grow and change in order to accomplish your dream?" "What will you become on your journey?" Any worthy goal involves change. If you don't think you'll have to grow and change, then you don't have a very inspiring goal. A worthy goal involves risk. It involves getting out of our comfort zone. That's where real growth occurs.

 So the short version of our conversation goes like this: what do you want, why do you want it and what are you willing to do to get it? These are questions you need to constantly be asking yourself.

If you do—if you take the time to think and ponder the answers, you'll gain greater clarity, more fulfillment, live longer and feel better. You will live a rich life.

 Richest Man in Babylon, by George Clason

Celebrating Success, by Gerard Smith

"A purpose to live for, a self to live with and a faith to live by."
—Bob Harrington

"Nothing contributes so much to tranquilizing the mind as a steady purpose—a point on which the soul may fix its intellectual eye."
—Mary Wollstonecraft Shelley

"Nothing can resist a human will that will stake even its existence on the extent of its purpose."
—Benjamin Disraeli

3.　The Blessing in Adversity

"The pessimist sees the difficulty in every opportunity;
the optimist, the opportunity in every difficulty."

When I was about five years old, I lived with my family in Enterprise, Alabama for a few months while my father attended an advanced aviation course at nearby Fort Rucker.

What makes Enterprise, Alabama especially memorable is a strange monument they have in the middle of town. You can't miss it. In fact, you have to drive around it because it sits right in the middle of the road. The monument is a statue to the boll weevil.

It's probably the only monument in the world erected in honor of an insect. It certainly wasn't done because of its aesthetic value—the boll weevil is a particularly ugly-looking creature. Surprisingly, it was erected because of the devastation the boll weevil caused to the cotton crops of the surrounding area.

Why did they honor this pest? Well, had it not been for the boll weevil, the local economy would have continued its unhealthy dependence on its one-crop, one-product economy.

Until then, everything depended entirely on cotton. When the boll weevil came, the farmers and all the other businesses that were reliant on the cotton farmers were forced to recognize the need to diversify.

In the long run, they saw that the boll weevil had, in fact, done them a favor by destroying their crops. No longer were their eggs all in one "cotton basket." They started raising hogs, peanuts and other cash crops, and the entire area was better off for it.

I think it is to those southern farmers' great credit that they were able to see this "adversity" for what it really was—a great blessing. Too often, we see difficult times as something to avoid—something only to endure. We usually don't see the benefit until much later—if at all.

If we look back at the things in our lives that were the most trying, the most painful and frustrating, we have to admit that there was value in it. If you can't see this, you're either too close to the situation or are too upset to see clearly.

Our lives are far more enjoyable—certainly more instructional—if we view each thing that happens to us as just that—a happening.

Remember, it's not what happens *to* us, but our *response* to what happens to us that makes the difference in the quality of our lives. I believe that everything that happens can be a lesson; every adversity can be a blessing. The following story illustrates this well.

Anthony Burgess discovered he had a brain tumor and only six months to live when he was 40 years old. He was distressed that he had nothing to leave his wife who was soon to become a widow. He decided to write—something he'd always wanted to do. The potential royalty from a book was the only thing he could think of doing to leave any kind of financial security for his family.

By the end of the first year and with no certainty that he would ever be published, he finished five novels. But he did not die. His cancer went into remission and then disappeared altogether.

In his long and full life, Anthony Burgess went on to write more than 70 books. Without the death sentence from cancer, he might not have written anything.

 Next time things don't seem to be going the way you want, ask yourself what the *positive* aspect is. What's the benefit in the adversity?

You'll have greater enjoyment and learn more in the process.

"There is no education like adversity."

—Benjamin Disraeli

"Every adversity carries with it the seed of an equal or greater benefit."

—Napoleon Hill

"Adversity is the first path of truth."

—Lord Byron

"Adversity reveals genius; prosperity conceals it."

—Horace

4.   The Willingness to Be Unpopular

Fitting in can be very costly indeed.

We all want to be liked. Surely you remember how important this was in your youth. Junior and senior high school were probably one of the most difficult times in our lives in terms of fitting in and being accepted. Virtually everything teenagers do is about being or becoming "cool."

Part of us never outgrows this. The desire to be popular and accepted runs deep.

Being a leader requires that we not always take the popular road. It demands making tough and often unpopular decisions—decisions that we'll be criticized for and perhaps even condemned. It's not easy.

It's not a whole lot different than being a good parent. If we wanted our children to like us all the time—to think we're "cool" and "hip"—we wouldn't be providing the best environment for them, and they wouldn't respect us.

Being a good parent and a good leader means we must look at the whole picture, take the long view and not be swayed by what others—our kids or those we supervise—think of us at the moment. It means being unpopular, and few people have the stomach for it.

Politics is a place we see this played out often. The power of the press and the clamor of the crowd will many times unnerve a statesman to the point they abandon their position and cave into the popular direction. I have a theory that our presidents would be better leaders if they were limited to only one term—perhaps six years. If that were the case, they would be making decisions they considered to be the best for the nation rather than the best for re-election.

A true leader doesn't disregard public opinion or the criticism and reproach of the press, but he doesn't let it run him either. He knows that if you're out front, people will shoot at you. He knows that the only way to avoid criticism is to say nothing, do nothing and be nothing.

And that is not his choice. The leader has a higher vision—a longer-term responsibility—and makes the tough decisions that most people aren't willing to make.

Integrity and values are critical here. As Zig Ziglar says, "The person who will not stand for something will fall for anything." If a leader caters too much to the crowd of public opinion, he will cease being a leader and will instead become a follower. When your values are strong and well-defined, it's hard to be unduly influenced by the masses.

One of my favorite quotes from *The Fountainhead*, Ayn Rand's classic novel of objectivism, is when Howard Roark says, "A building has integrity just like a man. And just as seldom."

It's no wonder many leaders are only recognized after they have lived. Lincoln was assassinated. Jesus was crucified. Sir Thomas Moore was beheaded. The list goes on.

Thankfully, we live in a time that it's unlikely our leadership will result in such violent endings. Even though it's improbable that we'll have to die for what we believe in, standing firm often means being ostracized.

If you aspire to being a leader—or a better one—remember you must be willing to be unpopular. If you need to be liked, if you crave admiration, you cannot be a real leader.

The road is narrow. The journey can be lonely. The rewards are great.

"The ultimate measure of a man is not where he stands in moments of comfort and convenience, but where he stands at times of challenge and controversy."

—Martin Luther King, Jr.

"Become the kind of leader that people would follow voluntarily, even if you had no title or position."

—Brian Tracy

5. Say Yes! or No!

*"Not all of us are going to be great orators and writers,
but being able to articulate our ideas intelligently is
critical to our success."*

The two most powerful words in any language are "yes" and "no."
They're often the first words we learn. They are powerful because
they are clear.

"Words," Rudyard Kipling once said, "are the most powerful drugs
used by mankind." I agree. And using the "right" words, the words
that express exactly what we want to say, is the key to effective
communication.

Words stir emotion and move people to action. People like Martin
Luther King, John Kennedy, Winston Churchill, Mother Teresa and
Abraham Lincoln were not given to vague, sloppy language. They
didn't use fluffy jargon. Their language was specific. It conveyed their
convictions and their feelings.

The English language contains more words than any other—over
600,000. German, a distant second, has only about half that
number. We certainly have no shortage of explicit words. And yet, we
seem to lack precise, powerful, clear communication.

In the midst of the information age, and with all the tools we have to
enhance communication, we still misunderstand one another far
more than is necessary. We experience it all the time—the missed
appointment, the job that needs to be redone, the hurt feelings—all
because what was said was not clearly understood.

A number of studies have revealed that a person's vocabulary has
more to do with income and position than almost anything else. It
has been documented that presidents of companies have a better
vocabulary than vice presidents and vice presidents have better
vocabularies than mid-level managers. It seems to hold true right
down the line. The ability to communicate well translates directly
into income and responsibility.

One of the first steps we can take to improve our ability to
communicate is simply to be clear on what it is we want to say.
What result do we intend? What is the essence of what we want to
communicate? It may seem ridiculous to offer this as a first step, but
often we start to say something without being clear ourselves on
what our intentions are.

Ambiguity and lazy language make poor use of our minds because our minds deal best with specifics. If you give yourself a specific objective and articulate it with precise words, the goal is already half accomplished.

There is something magical about a keen intention matched with clear communication. Perhaps they are the same thing.

I once heard someone say that if a man can't write his idea on the back of a business card, his idea isn't clearly enough defined. I think there's something to that.

It's true for organizations, also. An organization with a clear purpose and unclouded objectives will never be mediocre. This clarity is the beginning of excellence.

It's rare for people to just say yes or no. We seem to need to qualify our responses to the point that we dilute and weaken our meanings. Try just saying yes or no without qualifying or explaining. It's not easy, but it's *so* powerful.

Most of us have had the thrill of finding the perfect word or words to say exactly what we want. We know how to do it, but we're lazy. We've formed bad habits. Good communication takes conscious effort. It takes intention. It takes practice. It is, however, worth it.

 When you're about to start a meeting or begin a conversation with someone, ask yourself, "What do I want to say? What specific outcome do I want? How can I make myself easily understood?"

"Words form the thread on which we string our experiences."

—Aldous Huxley

"The difference between the right word and the wrong word is like the difference between lightning and the lightning bug."

—Mark Twain

"Kind words can be short and easy to speak, but their echoes are truly endless."

—Mother Teresa

6.   Leaders are Readers

Reading can be a powerful catalyst for thinking; it
has the potential for stimulating wisdom.

A long while ago, I heard someone say, "Leaders are readers." It
made a big impression on me, and I never forgot it. I don't know who
coined the phrase, but I must have reiterated it to my kids hundreds
of times. They would usually groan and roll their eyes. I doubted
that they really got it.

But a few years ago, my son in the Marine Corps shared with me the
long list of books he was planning to read on his upcoming deploy-
ment to the Far East and Africa. He told me he was on a "life-long
quest for knowledge." He said, "Dad, I remember what you used to
say, 'leaders are readers'".

I just stood there beaming. They really had heard me after all.
Thankfully, most of my children are avid readers. I hope that my
own example of reading constantly and my lessons on how "leaders
are readers" made a difference.

Of course, it doesn't follow that all *readers* are leaders, but I think
we can safely say with little exception, all *leaders* are readers.

If that's true, then why don't more people read?

I've learned that only ten percent of the people who begin reading a
nonfiction book ever get beyond the first chapter. It's been shown
that people's earnings are in direct proportion to their vocabularies.
That is, those who have larger vocabularies have greater responsibility and earn the most money—with very few exceptions. I know
for sure that most people want to earn more money, so why is it that
they don't study more?

In 1987, I was selling advertising for a business magazine I
published, and the upcoming issue focused on education (mostly
adult education). I called on a local businessman and told him about
the issue's focus, hoping to interest him in its wide appeal and
convince him it was a good investment of his advertising dollars. He
told me that he had already graduated from school, his education
was over and that he had no interest in education whatsoever.

I was dumbfounded. I think I could have comprehended someone
thinking that—but to actually *admit* it? A better salesman might have
tried a different tack, but I was so flabbergasted I just folded up my
things and left, shaking my head. Unfortunately, that attitude is far
more common than I realized.

Abraham Lincoln used to walk miles to borrow and return books. He read them by candlelight after working long, hard days. Do you think his reverence and devotion to books made a difference in his ability as a leader of our troubled nation? I do.

The good news is that people are reading more than they used to. Just look at the book stores and the vast number of books that are displayed on their shelves. *Somebody's* buying them! I'm encouraged by this. However, it's not enough.

I cannot go into a bookstore without buying a book. My personal library is my most valued material possession, and I take pride in adding to it regularly. I have over 500 nonfiction books. I've even read most of them. This should be true for any serious student of success.

If you're committed to be all that you are capable of being, I implore you to become a voracious reader. A book a month will keep you even. A book a year and you're falling behind.

It takes effort, but it's worth it. If you like to read—great—have at it. If you don't like reading—great—have at it. It's just something you have to do.

 Develop the habit of reading something every day. You will start to enjoy it. You'll look forward to it, your thinking will sharpen, your vocabulary will increase, and you'll become a more interesting person.

Remember, leaders are readers.

"No entertainment is so cheap as reading nor any pleasure so lasting."

—Mary Wortley Montagu

"Reading furnishes the mind only with materials of knowledge; it is thinking that makes what we read ours."

—John Locke

7.   Ten Thousand Failures

The "Wizard of Menlo Park" Saw Failure as Feedback

Thomas Edison once mentioned to reporters that he had tried over 10,000 materials as filaments for his new invention, the electric light bulb. One reporter asked how the young inventor maintained his persistence in the face of so much failure. "Failure?" he responded. "I didn't fail. What I did was successfully eliminate 10,000 elements which were unacceptable for my needs."

What most people would call failure, Edison saw as the process of invention.

The ability to accept so-called failure simply as information and then make corrections without self-invalidation is rare. However, it's a critical key to success. Accepting defeat or criticism is never easy, but it's those people who take feedback and make corrections who create lasting success.

Everyone Fails

Everyone makes mistakes and has painful experiences. Most people just complain about them, justify them or blame someone else. The self-actualized person learns from them, adjusts and goes on. No self-condemnation. No pity parties. No blame. Just awareness and correction. It's not what happens to us but rather what we do with what happens to us that makes the difference.

How do we make corrections without self-invalidation? Here's an example: If we were to fly to a distant city, our flight would be off course more than 90 percent of the time. Constant feedback and correction would be required to reach our intended destination. As we drift off course, the guidance system reports to the autopilot, and the autopilot makes the necessary adjustments. As our altitude drops or increases slightly, the same thing occurs. This feedback and correction cycle continues over and over again hundreds of thousands of times throughout the course of our flight.

Can you imagine such an exchange of information between two people? After about the hundredth time, the pilot would probably lose it with the navigator. "Stop it! Just shut up and leave me alone. I'm doing my job!"

But the autopilot never gets angry at the guidance system for its constant correction and the guidance system never makes the autopilot wrong for being off course. It is the ultimate in correction without invalidation.

We Can All Learn from this Analogy

Being off course doesn't mean we are wrong or bad. It's just information that we can use to make a correction.

Many of us use computers. When we don't get the results we want, we often blame the computer. But usually the problem is not in the hardware; it's in the programs or in the instructions we give it.

The computer can be flawless, but if the instructions are faulty, the intended outcome will be undesirable. Although we may get frustrated with computers and with ourselves for errors, it's counterproductive to blame the system or ourselves.

Like computers, we humans often run programs (belief systems and strategies) which result in failure. We frequently make ourselves wrong for being less than perfect. We berate ourselves for our mistakes or don't admit our mistakes because that would mean we're bad. We spend huge quantities of emotional energy in justifying or feeling guilty rather than looking for different approaches that will bring success. To overcome adversity, we must redirect this energy in better ways.

Self-invalidation is a Debilitating Disease

It keeps us from accomplishing much that we would attempt if we weren't so afraid of failing—of being wrong. More is lost from not doing something than from trying and failing. The price of doing nothing is high. The money you don't make is more than the money you may lose.

As Robert Schuller asks, "What great thing would you attempt if you knew you couldn't fail?" It's worth serious contemplation because, in fact, there is no failure.

 Like Edison, view your errors as part of the process of success. If you learn to embrace them and use them, they can become your tools instead of your enemies.

"Honest criticism is hard to take, particularly from a relative, a friend, an acquaintance or a stranger."

—Franklin P. Jones

8. Building People Up

By its very definition, leadership requires followers. To become a good leader, it's necessary to bring people along with you and to help build them into better people—often, to train them as leaders.

How is this done? First, it's important to have a clear and worthwhile vision. Certainly this will help to attract devoted followers.

Integrity is also critical in building loyalty.

But becoming a builder of people requires more. It takes a genuine desire and commitment to call forth the best in others—to believe in them, even when they may doubt themselves.

People are Everything

Too often, people are looked upon as being easily replaceable and yet, in every successful organization, people are put first.

Andrew Carnegie, the great steel magnate, once said, "If you take away all my mills and all my capital, but leave me with my people, I will have it all rebuilt in a short while." Many business leaders today are questioning the old adage that the "customer is number one," and now say the "*employee* is number one." If you take good care of your people, your customers will automatically be well taken care of.

Being a powerful leader does not mean people will follow you blindly, although there are certainly examples of that in history. The intention is not to become a guru; it's to become more like a shepherd—one who cares for, nurtures and watches over his flock. The objective should not be to feed the ego and denigrate the masses, it should be to accomplish the vision and lift everyone else in the process.

Shoulder the Blame and Share the Glory

One of the things that separates a true leader from a wannabe is that of acknowledgment. You can tell by the speech the captain of the team gives when he accepts the trophy: If he takes all the credit and doesn't share it with his team, he's not a leader. A real leader always gives credit to everyone who made it happen.

Conversely, when things go wrong and victory slips away, the builder of people answers the charge. When John F. Kennedy shouldered the blame for the Bay of Pigs fiasco, he said, "I take full responsibility." That was the day, in my eyes, he became a true leader.

It's easy to underestimate the value and power of lauding people for their accomplishments. We forget how just one genuine compliment made to someone at the right time can make all the difference. That one comment may be remembered for years to come and could play a major role in that person's self-esteem and confidence. Praising someone is easy to do and so often forgotten. It costs so little; yet the return is enormous.

Criticism and Praise

Much damage has been done by people in authority (teachers, parents, bosses, coaches and the like) who chastise someone publicly for some shortcoming or wrongdoing. In many instances, it has resulted in the broken spirit of a child or even an adult. There is a time for criticism and a time for praise. The first should be done only in private and the second done publicly.

Most of the time, criticism is unnecessary. By focusing on what works, the things that *don't* work will often go away. Tom Peters likes to say, "Catch people doing things *right!*"

Create Safety

A good leader makes it safe to ask questions and make mistakes. The builder of people is approachable and easy to talk to. There are never any stupid questions and mistakes are not only tolerated, but are treated as a necessary process on the way to success.

There's a story about a top executive at IBM who was in charge of a project that ended in disaster, causing the company ten million dollars in losses.

The executive met with the president to go over what went wrong, expecting the worse. "I suppose you want my resignation," he stammered. "On the contrary," said the president, "we just spent ten million dollars educating you. Do you think we want to lose that kind of investment?"

There's no doubt in my mind that experience went a long way in building a valuable and productive leader for "Big Blue."

 There may not be any such thing as constructive criticism. You are not perfect, nor will you ever be. If you constantly look to build on your own strengths and the strengths of others, you'll go far. If you look for the best in people, you're likely to find it.

9. A Global Network

How to Cash in on the New International Currency

Any banker will tell you—if they're completely honest—that your greatest financial asset is your ability to earn income. It's not your house, your bank accounts or your car. They don't actually want your collateral, they want your payments. What's important to them is your ability to earn money on an ongoing basis. That ability is based on your health (your capacity to work), your knowledge, your skills, your reputation and your experience.

It's also based on who you know.

It's always been that way. Have you ever closed a sale simply because you had an existing relationship with your buyer? Conversely, you've probably lost a sale or an account because your prospect went to the same fraternity as your competitor or something similar.

It might not be fair, but it's the way things work. You can lament the unfairness of the setup or you can make it work for you. And with today's technology, you can network globally, and work with people you haven't even met face to face.

No matter how technically savvy we become, business still comes down to relationships. People like doing business with people they know and like. Who you know and how well you know them counts for as much—if not more—than *what* you know and how good your product/service is.

In my studies of successful people, I've found that every one of them can attribute a large portion of their achievement to the help of and association with other people. They were led to someone who could help them and they did. People like to help others—they really do. When it comes to networking, the words of Zig Ziglar were never more true, "You can get anything you want in life if you will just help enough other people get what they want."

And that's what it's about—helping other people. No matter what you do for work—whether you realize it or not—you're in the networking business. When you network people together, everyone wins—you and the people whom you connect.

Most of them will appreciate and remember what you've done for them and return the favor. The idea is to develop a global network of people and organizations—one that you'll continue to build upon and that will help you throughout your career.

When you leave your present position, your contact list can be your ticket to a new job and/or new business. I recommend you keep your own contact list and not rely upon that of your employer. In fact, you could even be sued by your former employer if they feel you've taken lists and information that was proprietary.

I keep track of everyone I meet. It takes only a moment to enter their names, address and telephone information, as well as a couple of personal notes about them. I track them for two reasons: what I might do for them and what they might do for me. Be sure to exchange business cards with everyone with whom you come in contact.

Your contact list—your network of coworkers, business associates, friends, golfing buddies and the like is a gold mine. Treat it like one, and you'll have an abundant supply of the New International Currency.

 You must work your list. Maintain contact. Networking is a contact sport. Call people. Send them referrals. Mail copies of articles they'd find interesting. If you want to build and maintain relationships, you have to be proactive.

 The World's Best Known Marketing Secret, by Dr. Ivan Misner
Business Network Int'l
www.BNInet.com

"Some of the biggest challenges in relationships come from the fact that most people enter a relationship in order to get something: they're trying to find someone who's going to make them feel good. In reality, the only way a relationship will last is if you see your relationship as a place that you go to give, and not a place that you go to take."

—Tony Robbins

10. The Eleventh Commandment

"Thou Shalt Not Should on Thyself (or others)."

I've spent far too many years of my life caring too much about what other people thought. I was a magnet for people telling me what to do. And I let them "should" on me—a lot. As a result, I made some very poor decisions based upon "expert" advice that was totally contrary to what I knew in my heart was the right thing to do.

When someone I cared about would give me advice, I felt bad if I didn't follow their recommendation. Maybe I just didn't trust myself enough to follow my heart—or didn't know how. I found it easy to feel guilty about what I did or didn't do—simply because it didn't match the views of others I respected.

Most everyone has an opinion about what you should do. It takes a strong resolve to become clear and stay true to your inner guidance system. It's one of the toughest things to learn.

I had to become aware that guilt was literally running my life. It took several years and some painful mistakes to overcome allowing guilt to plague me, but I did.

Like everyone, I've made mistakes and sometimes even hurt people I didn't intend to. But I've hurt myself and others far more by trying to please people than by not. Herbert Bayard Swope said, "I cannot give you a formula for success, but I can give you a formula for failure which is: Try to please everybody." Staying true to yourself isn't easy, but I think it's the only way to live.

Many people feel shame for no reason other than the misplaced opinion of others. They feel bad because of mistakes they've made and because of the "shoulds" of others. Feeling bad doesn't accomplish anything. Guilt has no virtue. Operating out of obligation and guilt lacks integrity. Don't do it.

No one can walk in your shoes. No one can live your life. Ultimately, it's you who must answer to how you've lived. We all need to learn the art of correction without invalidation—to see our errors, learn from them and move on—without self-condemnation.

If you feel remorse about something you've done or failed to do, take action. If you can make amends, do so. If you can't, forgive yourself and move on. Vow not to make the same mistake again. If God can forgive you (most religions teach that He does), then you can forgive yourself.

I'm not saying that you should (there's that word again) totally disregard the information and advice put to you. I'm simply suggesting that you evaluate the information, listen carefully to your heart and do what you think is right. Just because someone is a travel agent for guilt trips doesn't mean you have to buy their tickets.

"I have met the enemy; and it is the eyes of other people."

—Ben Franklin

"You are your own authority. Choose not to be affected by the negative opinions or attitudes of others."

—unknown

"When the freedom they wished for most was freedom from responsibility, then Athens ceased to be free and was never free again."

—Edith Hamilton

"A 'should' is a 'have to' with no teeth; it is dead energy."

—Ruth Ross

11. Going For It

*"Most people look to avoid risk;
the greater risk is not going for it."*

I've always been fascinated by stories of spectacular achievement. My library is filled with books about people of great accomplishment. It's easy to admire those who have overcome difficult circum- stances—people who have taken great risks and won.

What's really important, though, is what we can learn from these people we so revere. If we can't benefit from their success, then we've missed some of the purpose of their having lived, struggled and triumphed.

We can use these success stories to increase the belief that we, too, can accomplish great things—and we surely can.

If my studies of great men and women have taught me anything, it's that they weren't really all that different from the rest of us. It's just that what they wanted to accomplish was more important to them than their own doubts and fears. Their circumstances weren't all that much different.

Their talents weren't always superior. They were just willing to give their all—to go for it—full on, 100 percent, no matter what.

If there is so much veneration for those who go for the brass ring, why are there so few people willing to take the risk? One of the reasons is that we care too much about what others think.

The I-told-you-sos and knew-it-wouldn't-works are always going to be around. I call them dream killers. Perhaps they're placed here to test whether or not we're really serious about our goals.

Where do *you* stand on the "go-for-it scale?" What dream lies hidden away that you long to fulfill? Will you keep it buried inside and end up like those poor souls who Oliver Wendell Holmes was talking about when he wrote, "Alas for those who never sing, but die with all their music in them?" Or will you be one of the few who stake everything on the accomplishment of your purpose?

There's often great risk and pain involved in going for your dreams. But if it were easy, then everyone would do it. It wouldn't be exceptional. There's risk either way. And I think there's even greater risk and suffering in *not* going for it.

No doubt about it, putting yourself out there and telling the world what you're going to do is scary! What if you don't succeed and everyone sees you fail? What then? The truth is, most people don't think about you anywhere near as much as *you* might think.

Most people think of themselves. And, oftentimes, the people who are the most critical are usually secretly wishing they had the guts to do what you're doing.

I know what it's like to fail. I've fallen out of the sky several times, but I'd rather crash and burn than wear myself out sitting on the runway trying to get up enough courage to take off.

It's more fun, too! Sure it hurts to fail, but it hurts more to live with the feelings of knowing you were not willing to try.

Helen Keller said, "Security is mostly superstition. It does not exist in nature nor do the children of man as a whole experience it. Avoiding danger is no safer in the long run than outright exposure. Life is either a daring adventure, or nothing."

Life's a risk. In fact, it's so risky we're not going to get out alive. If we knew the outcome of everything, if everything turned out just the way we wanted, it would be boring. There would be no fun and no adventure.

 In the words of Goethe, "Whatever you can do or dream you can, begin it. Boldness has genius, magic and power in it."

Don't wait for the perfect time. It won't ever come.

Go for it now!

"The irony is that the person not taking risks feels the same amount of fear as the person who regularly takes risks."

—Peter McWilliams

"Progress always involves risk; you can't steal second base and keep your foot on first."

—Frederick Wilcox

"Today, you have 100% of your life left."

—Tom Hopkins

12. Position Yourself for Success

"Just like in a race or game of chess, you must position yourself to make the right move. By being in the right place at the right time, you can dramatically increase your chances for success in any endeavor."

In the spring of 1940, Winston Churchill was asked to lead Great Britain in its defense against Germany. Few could argue that Churchill was the right person for the job.

He later wrote, "I felt as if I were walking with destiny, and that all my past life had been but a preparation for this hour and for this trial." The new Prime Minister became one of the greatest statesmen in world history. He helped England successfully resist and (with the help of the U.S.) eventually defeat the Nazi war machine.

He was prepared for leadership.

We don't have control over what happens *to* us. We do have a great deal of control over how we prepare ourselves and position ourselves for reaching our goals.

There may be times in our lives when the path ahead is unclear—when we're not quite sure of which direction we should choose. If this is the case, we can always prepare for that time when we *are* clear and we *do* know exactly what to do. This can be a valuable time of preparation. And it can pay big dividends. Oftentimes, merely the process of preparation—the activity itself—will provide clarity and certainty as to our plans.

I recommend you use the following checklist to improve your personal positioning. How do you rate in each area? What can you do to enhance your preparedness?

1. **Health and Vitality.** You can't have get-up-and-go if you don't have a reserve of energy and good health. We must take care of ourselves in order to have the drive and strength to go after our dreams. You know what to do. It's common sense. Eat right, get adequate rest, and take good care of your body. It's the only one you get.

2. **Education and Skills.** What you know and what you can do in terms of skills is a big part of your positioning. What skills do you need to work on? What do you need to learn? Take some classes. Do some research. Read. Make a commitment to a life-long search for knowledge and upgrading your skills. It will not

only increase your preparation quotient, but it will keep you feeling stimulated—even young.

3. **Contacts.** The people you know and the relationships you've developed over the years can be a virtual gold mine to you. It's imperative you cultivate and build your associations in order to obtain help and round up talent for your projects.

4. **Self-Image and Self-Esteem.** How you feel about yourself comes across to others. It can't be faked. You increase your self-esteem by doing the right thing—always. You improve your confidence by doing what you say you'll do—whether you say it to yourself or to others. Every time we lie, we chip away at our self-image.

   There is no status quo. We either build or tear down our self-esteem. Integrity is the essence of everything successful.

5. **Finances and Credit.** Most opportunities involve an investment of money as well as time and energy. Having money in the bank and good credit on which to borrow can go a long way toward tipping the scales in your favor. In the world of business, "cash is king." Pay off those debts and create some savings (if you haven't already) and get ready.

6. **Attitude**. People with good attitudes not only get more done, they attract opportunity and people who can help them.

   Are you someone people like to be around? Would you consider your attitude to be one of your strongest assets? Regardless of your answer, you can improve your attitude and along with it, your success.

   Read good books. Listen to good tapes. Stay around positive people. Study people you think have good attitudes and emulate that part of them.

It's not easy, I know. As Coach Bear Bryant said, "It's not the will to win, but the will to *prepare* to win that makes the difference."

"Thorough preparation makes its own luck."

—Joe Poyer

"I would as soon appear before an audience half clothed as half prepared."

—Daniel Webster

13. The Lost Art of Thinking

Auguste Rodin's classic statue "The Thinker" is one of my favorites. It's hard to look at it (or one of its many replicas) without being moved by it. The innocent display of someone deeply in thought causes most of us to ponder a bit ourselves. Why is this image so captivating? What's he thinking about?

Perhaps we have such reverence for this kind of deep thinking because it's so uncommon. Having thoughts does not constitute thinking. We all have thoughts. We all have opinions and beliefs—usually lots of them.

William James once wrote, "A great many people think they are thinking when they are merely rearranging their prejudices." Just because there's mental activity going on in our minds doesn't mean we're thinking.

Bob Proctor, in his book *You Were Born Rich* writes, "Thinking is the highest function of which a human being is capable." He goes on to say that what passes for thinking for most people is really just the faculty of memory—playing old movies and rehashing past events. I doubt this is what Rodin's great work of art depicts.

Thinking is hard work. Maybe that's why so few people do it. Edison went even further: "There is no expedient to which a man will go to avoid the real labor of thinking." And Emerson, "What is the hardest task in the world? To think."

Why don't we think more? I believe one reason is that we're so busy *doing*, we don't take time to conceive, cogitate and consider. We're used to being entertained. We're bombarded with information. It comes at us so fast, we have little time to reflect on it.

From TV commentators to politicians, we're told *what* to think when what we really need to know is *how* to think. We've become accustomed to quick answers and easy solutions. But the problems and challenges of our lives are not easy, and they're not simple. They require thoughtful consideration.

I love to read. And I'm convinced the greatest value in reading is not the information you obtain, but rather what you *think* about while you read (that's why what you choose to read is so important).

The objective is not to fill our minds with information, but to stimulate our mind to think and to ponder. The value of the book is increased a thousand fold if we lay it down occasionally, contemplate what we've read and think about what it means and how and why it might apply to us.

Clarity is power. And clarity comes from thinking.

 You need to think, and think carefully about the choices and direction of your life. The most precious resource you have is your time. Your life is the sum total of what you do with that time. Isn't it worth spending more of it thinking?

Think about it.

<hr/>

"We are what we think. All that we are arises with our thoughts. With our thoughts, we make our world."

—The Buddha

"No problem can stand the assault of sustained thinking."

—Voltaire

"To think is to practice brain chemistry."

—Deepak Chopra

14. Entrepreneurs and *Intrepreneurs*

The dictionary defines an entrepreneur as a person who organizes, operates and assumes the risk for a business venture.

Our New Economy demands an entrepreneurial spirit.

It used to be that employers didn't want entrepreneurs working for them. They were afraid the entrepreneurial type would leave after being trained up—perhaps even become a competitor.

Today, progressive employers want entrepreneurs on their staff. They might not refer to them as entrepreneurs, but that's what they are.

I call them *in*trepreneurs—men and women who harbor the entrepreneurial spirit while working *in* a larger organization.

As more and more good people leave the W-2 world to become free agents, talent, ambition and experience will be that much more in demand. The wise employer will encourage an independent entrepreneurial spirit.

The employer of the next century will look for ways to attract and nurture their existence. He or she will set up win-win relationships that allow for independent contracts.

What we really want to do is treat our job like it was our own business. In doing so, we maximize our value to our employer and at the same time maximize our individual value.

What are some of the qualities of an entrepreneur? Here are a few:

Vision. An entrepreneur sees what is not yet there. They have the ability to envision something different, something better.

Creativity. Someone with an entrepreneurial mind is innovative. They can take circumstances or pieces of information and reorder them to make something completely different.

Persistence. Entrepreneurs are self-starters. They don't need a lot of supervision or much structure. They have stick-to-it-iveness. They work hard and get things done.

Resilience. Entrepreneurs are resilient. They get back up after being knocked down. Entrepreneurs aren't easily discouraged and they don't quit.

Goal Setting. Entrepreneurs know the principles of goal setting. They have measurable objectives, are clear on what they want, determine the obstacles to getting there and have a plan of action to accomplish their goals.

Passion. An entrepreneur loves what they do, and the quality of their work shows it. They have passion for their industry, their business and their projects.

Change. The entrepreneurial type leverages change. They seem to thrive on chaos. And turmoil will continue to be the norm.

Enthusiasm. A good entrepreneur has the ability to sell others on their ideas. They get others excited by their vision, their belief and their enthusiasm.

Risk. Entrepreneurs are risk-takers. They're not reckless; they take calculated risks. Security isn't something they need. They know that in life, there's no real security—only opportunity.

Entrepreneurs are made, not born. To paraphrase Zig Ziglar, we've never seen where an entrepreneur was born, but we've seen where they've died. So, somewhere between birth and death, by choice or by training, they became an entrepreneur.

 And so can you. By developing an entrepreneurial spirit, you'll become more successful, whether in your own business or someone else's organization. Your value will increase, your income will rise, and you will succeed.

"The five essential entrepreneurial skills for success: Concentration, Discrimination, Organization, Innovation and Communication."

—Michael Gerber

"The entrepreneur always searches for change, responds to it and exploits it as an opportunity."

—Peter Drucker

15. Improving Your Effectiveness

Ten Questions to Ask in Order
to Enhance Your Effectiveness

I believe that questions are the answers. What I mean is that the process of asking good questions—questions that lead to more clarity—lead us to power.

After all, isn't that what a good consultant or therapist does?

A good counselor doesn't give us the answers. They help us get clear on the problems we face and allow us to uncover how best to resolve them. Much of the value of a coach/consultant/therapist session is that we're forced to take the time to think and ponder the answers to good questions.

A great deal of this can be done by ourselves if we take the time to generate and consider elegant questions. By using these questions as a tool, they'll move you further along the path of success, and you'll have a more fulfilling journey.

1. **What is my purpose? My mission?** We need a mission that motivates and inspires us to be our best. Is mine clear? Does it empower me? Do I feel impassioned by it?

2. **What are my three most important goals right now?** These should be at our top-of-mind awareness. These goals must be measurable, personal and have a target date for completion.

3. **What actions can I take today to move me closer to accomplishing these three goals?** Actions are just that—measurable steps over which we have control. Do it now!

4. **What are my three biggest roadblocks to accomplishing my three most important goals?** What are my biggest problems? What stops me? What discourages me? What do I need in order to get the job done?

5. **What can I set in motion today?** Too many people wait for their ship to come in when they've never sent any out. What can I cause to happen? What can I begin today? Remember, beginning is half done.

6. **What can I complete today?** Completions empower. We can't be totally present unless our past is fully complete. Those things left undone drag us down and hinder our progress. Check something off today. Put it behind you. "Do it, dump it or change it."

7. **What are three things I'm now tolerating and want to eliminate?** We get what we settle for. By getting rid of what we *don't* want in our lives, we make way for what we *do* want. It's the principle of vacuum. By eliminating our tolerations, we free up our energy, reduce our frustration and increase our creativity.

8. **Who and what am I most appreciative of in my life?** Another meaning of the word appreciate is to increase in value or price. An attitude of gratitude is worthy of cultivation. By focusing on what/who we have in our lives, we'll eventually have even more to appreciate.

9. **If I had six months to live, what would I do with it?** We each have 100% of the rest of our lives left. But the fact is, we may not even have six months to live. Shouldn't we live the next six months as if they were our last?

10. **What are the three most important things in the world to me?** We love what we give our time to. Am I giving my time (loving) what's really important to me?

"You can tell whether a man is clever by his answers. You can tell whether a man is wise by his questions."

—Naguib Mahfouz

"You can see a lot just by looking."

—Yogi Berra

16. Kicking the Worry Habit

"Worry is like prayer in reverse."

I grew up on a Vermont farm. After college, I bought a farm of my own and operated it for several years. During this time, I learned the secret to making a small fortune in farming. It's kind of inside information, and I don't pass it around to just anybody. Ready? Here it is: start out with a large one. And sooner or later, you'll have a small one.

Farmers don't lead easy lives. The work is hard and the risks are great. They're dependent on the weather and many other things outside of their control.

I used to worry all the time. I worried about livestock disease. I worried about getting bank loans. I worried about the buying price of grain and the selling price of livestock. I worried about not having enough money. I was unhappy, fatigued and irritable. It had become a disease.

And then I read Dale Carnegie's classic, *How to Stop Worrying and Start Living*. In doing so, I realized I was making myself sick with worry, and I could pay a very heavy price. Reading that book may have saved my life.

I came to the awareness that worry is like prayer in reverse. When we worry and fret over things, we make them bigger than they really are, as well as attract what we're fussing over. It's positive proof of the principle of visualization—only in a negative way.

Somehow, I had it wired up that worry was actually virtuous. I guess I figured I wasn't being a good parent unless I worried about my kids. I thought I was being irresponsible if I wasn't worrying about my business and my finances. Not so.

It took me over a year to kick the worry habit. It wasn't easy. It took daily diligence to eradicate it from my life. I occasionally slip back into worry for brief periods, but I don't stay with it. It no longer runs my life.

Worry is not our friend; it's our enemy. Jim Rohn says, "Worry is like an economic cancer. And if continued, it will haul you off into a financial desert where you will choke on the dust of your own regrets." How's that for a vivid picture?

Most of the things we worry about are things over which we have little or no control. If we think about it, it's stupid. Agonizing about what might occur and about things we can't control gives away our power.

Thankfully, most of what we worry about never occurs. The French philosopher Michel Eyquem de Montaigne wrote in the 1500's, "My life has been filled with terrible misfortune; most of which never happened."

What do *you* worry about? In my research, I've found most people are excellent worriers. They worry about illness, lack of money, old age, taxes, the next generation—you name it!

They burn up their energy, lower their resistance to illness and actually draw to them what they fear. Like Job in the Bible, "That which I have feared has come upon me."

Our hospitals and cemeteries are filled with people who made worry an everyday companion. Don't be one of them. If you suffer from this affliction, you need to cure yourself.

By doing so, you'll be healthier, live longer, have more fun and produce more of what you want.

 The biggest lever for change is to be aware of what you're doing and realize how detrimental it is to your life. If you find yourself upset or anxious, check to see if you're worrying. If so, focus on what you *want* rather than what you *don't* want.

You can't simply *stop* worrying. You have to *replace* your worry by thinking about desired results—something good instead of something bad. Start working on the solution rather than a possible negative outcome.

"If you believe that feeling bad or worrying long enough will change a fact, then you are residing on another planet with a different reality system."

—Wayne Dyer

"Men do not die from overwork. They die from dissipation and worry."
—Charles Evans Hughes

"Worry is simply an unhealthy and destructive mental habit."
—Norman Vincent Peale

17. Visualize Your Success

How Visualization Can Become Reality

If you've had any kind of exposure to success technologies, you've certainly heard about the power of visualization.

Well, it's true. It works. We attract what we think about. And we do it all the time—consciously or unconsciously. The key is to direct our visualization in a positive rather than a negative fashion—to take charge of what we visualize in order to attract what we want.

Following is one of the best stories I've heard of the power of directed visualization.

Major James Nesmeth was just an average weekend golfer, shooting in the mid- to low-nineties. Then, because of events beyond his control, he stopped playing for seven years. Never touched a club. Never set foot on a fairway.

When he did start playing again, he shot an astonishing 74! He'd knocked 20 strokes off his average without having swung a golf club in seven years! For those of you who don't play golf, this is an astonishing feat for any golfer. For someone who hadn't even played, it's unbelievable. Not only that, but Major Nesmeth's physical condition had greatly deteriorated during his golfing sabbatical.

You see, Major Nesmeth had spent those seven years as a prisoner of war in North Vietnam. During almost the entire time he was imprisoned, he saw no one, talked to no one and experienced no physical activity. He realized he had to find a way to keep his mind occupied or he'd lose his sanity. To save his life, he learned to visualize.

In his mind, he selected his favorite country club and started to play. Every day, he played a full 18 holes at this imaginary golf course. He experienced everything in great detail. He saw himself dressed in his golfing clothes. He smelled the fragrance of the trees and the newly trimmed grass. He imagined different weather conditions—windy spring days, overcast winter afternoons and sunny summer mornings.

It took him as long in imaginary time to play 18 holes as it would have taken in reality. Not a detail was omitted. Seven days a week. Four hours a day. Eighteen holes.

And after seven years, he shot a 74.

Our subconscious minds can't tell the difference between reality and what we vividly imagine. It's a powerful thing indeed.

Many people don't consciously visualize on a regular basis. They think they can't do it right, so they figure, why bother. But like anything else, it takes practice. The more you do it, the better you get. The payoff is substantial.

Whenever you have doubts about its benefit, remember the story of Major Nesmeth.

 Picture what you want. Imagine all the details. Use all of your senses. Fill your mind with a vibrant, real picture of your success. You get what you focus on, so focus on your success.

———⊂////⊃———

"I've got vision and the rest of the world wears bifocals."
—the movie, Butch Cassidy and the Sundance Kid

"A vision without a task is but a dream. A task without a vision is drudgery. A vision with a task is the hope of the world."
—Inscription from a church in Sussex, England, 1730

18. How to Stay Motivated

A Purpose to Live For, A Self to Live With
and a Faith to Live By

What motivates you? How do *you* stay focused?

We're all motivated a little differently. Some of us are turned on by money—or rather what we think the money will do for us. Others are motivated by ego and the drive for glory. Sometimes, we're motivated by fear—of loss, of death, of loneliness and a host of other things. Still others are driven by the desire to help people.

What we need is drive that doesn't drive us over the edge. We need motivation that keeps us going through the discouraging times. We need motivation that enables us to consistently do what we know we need to do and then to do it at a level of excellence of which we can be proud.

I can't say what will work for you, but I'd like to share what's worked for me in my 50-plus trips around the sun. These are what I call the three keys to developing sustained motivation.

Key 1: A Purpose to Live For

First and foremost in staying motivated is to have a strong purpose. One person with a dream can accomplish more than 100 others without one. If you have a burning desire, you can accomplish anything. The biographies of great men and women are full of stories of how they did seemingly impossible things because they had a dream.

Much of the time, people are expending too much effort working on the "how," when what they really need to focus on is the "why." If you don't have a strong enough reason, you won't find out what you need to know, you won't do the things you need to do, when you need to do them.

We're either motivated by moving away from something or moving toward something. Each can be a driving force, but I believe moving toward a worthy purpose will provide the greatest fulfillment.

One of the most important things you can do to ensure your success is to be clear on your life purpose.

Key 2: A Self to Live With

Too many times, I've seen people doing the right things and even doing them for good reasons, but they self-destruct because they don't feel worthy. They've taken shortcuts. They've not done the little things that add up to being a big person.

When the person we are and the person we "appear" to be are inconsistent, we're at cross purposes to ourselves—we're out of integrity. And as Bucky Fuller said, "Integrity is the essence of everything successful."

Fanny Brice said it quite eloquently, "Let the world know you as you are, not as you think you should be—because sooner or later, if you're posing, you will forget the pose and then where are you?" It takes far too much energy to be someone other than who you are— so just be yourself. Besides, there's nobody better qualified.

We must learn to appreciate and accept ourselves. In doing so, we can love and accept others more easily.

Key 3: A Faith to Live By

I've never met or studied anyone, whom I would consider to be successful, who did not have strong faith. To have sustained motivation, it's necessary to have a powerful faith—in yourself, in your product, in your team, in your purpose—in something greater than yourself.

I think that developing this faith is best done with quiet intro-spection, by listening and by being open to a higher power and presence—what Napoleon Hill called "Infinite Intelligence."

When I'm in tune with this Infinite Wisdom, my life works. When I'm not, it doesn't. When I'm "in the flow," things seem to come to me with ease. "Coincidences" happen that don't seem to occur when I'm operating separately.

It hasn't always been the case, but I've learned to love myself even when I screw up. I don't spend much time at pity parties feeling sorry for myself. I've learned to accept and even laugh at my failings and then look for what they can teach me.

I realize that I won't ever fully accomplish my purpose. That's why I will never retire. I fully expect to live to be 120 years old in good health. And if I died tomorrow, I would make my transition knowing that I'm living my life on purpose. That keeps me at peace. It keeps me motivated.

19. Positive Thinking

A few years back, I was asked to present a series of workshops to some high-school seniors on the subject of Positive Thinking.

It's a subject that's near and dear to my heart, but I approached the assignment with some trepidation. The idea of leading a group of seventeen- and eighteen-year-olds for fifty minutes was for some reason more challenging than speaking to adults.

What Exactly is Positive Thinking?

Why is it important? How do you develop it? How do you keep a positive attitude in the face of negative circumstances?

And these kids expected answers. It caused me to do some real soul searching as to what I think a PMA (positive mental attitude) is and how to apply it in our lives.

To me, Positive Thinking means a "can-do" attitude—an attitude that allows one to see the best in all circumstances. It means facing a given situation and looking for the opportunities that almost always lie within. It's really a matter of focus. It's a little bit like when you're buying a new car and you notice all the cars on the road like the one you're buying. They were always there before, but you just didn't notice them because you weren't looking for them. When you're looking for good, you'll certainly find it. That's Positive Thinking.

Positive thinking is not Pollyanna Thinking. Being a "Permagrinner" is almost as bad as being a negative thinker. It's an unwillingness to see things as they are and ignore the things that could present a danger to us and our well-being.

We need to be realistic and address the problems with which we're faced. If you're tending a garden and ignore the weeds, you'll find your garden over-run by them. You have to be aware and take care of problems. Positive Thinking is definitely not avoidance.

Negative thinking is all too common. It doesn't take any effort to be a negative thinker. I call them "Stinking Thinkers"—people with Mental BO. You know the kind of people I'm talking about—the kind of people who brighten up a room—by *leaving*. They're cynical and depressing to be around. They complain too much and offer too little, if any, help.

Positive Thinking is infectious. Unfortunately, so is negative thinking. Emerson wrote, "A man becomes what he thinks about all day long." What do you think about? Where's your focus? Do you dwell on your problems, or do you focus on the way you'd like them resolved? It's your perspective that determines whether the glass is half full or half empty.

Our attitude affects people more than we may realize. When we approach problems with enthusiasm and high expectations, and when we share our optimism, we cause others to look at things in new and more optimistic ways. We help shift their perspective.

When I'm hiring someone, I place more weight on their attitude than on their skills and knowledge. Skills and knowledge can always be learned. Positive Thinking can be learned too, but I find few people willing to develop it. The belief is often, "that's-just-the-way-I-am."

How Do We Develop a Positive Attitude?

One way is to associate with positive people. We may have to change our environment and even choose new friends. This may seem drastic, but you can't afford to be with people who drag you down. In order to be successful, you have to have a supportive atmosphere.

We can also read good books. You might want to start with Norman Vincent Peale's classic, *The Power of Positive Thinking.* He coined the acronym and phrase "PMA." Any book that is encouraging, inspiring and positive will do.

No matter how good your PMA might be, it takes constant attention. You eat every day, don't you? Your attitude is like your body; it needs to be nourished. You need to feed it with good, healthy food—positive people, good books and an inspiring environment. Just like you go to work every day, you need to go to work on yourself every day. If you do, you'll build and maintain a Positive Mental Attitude.

"If you realized how powerful your thoughts are, you would never think a negative thought."

—Peace Pilgrim

"I am optimistic and confident in all that I do. I affirm only the best for myself and others. I am the creator of my life and my world. I meet daily challenges gracefully and with complete confidence. I fill my mind with positive, nurturing and healing thoughts."

—Alice Potter

20. The Meaning of Success

I once got a letter from a high school student in Australia. He wanted to know my definition of success. It's a good question, and I thought I'd share my answer with you.

Most people will tell you that they want to be a success. But it's a rare individual who can tell you what that means. Studies show fewer than ten percent of North Americans consider themselves to be successful. Less than ten percent!

Only three percent say they feel truly successful. It's interesting to note that ten percent have clearly defined goals and about three percent have written their goals down. I wonder if there's any correlation.

Why is there such a discrepancy between those who want to succeed and those who feel they're unsuccessful? First of all, success isn't easy. Another reason so few people consider themselves successful is that success is so misunderstood and poorly defined, it's difficult to tell whether we are or aren't. How would we know?

Paul J. Meyer, president of Success Motivation Institute, says, "Success is the progressive realization of worthwhile, predetermined personal goals."

Let's take a close look at this definition because it's a good one.

Progressive means ongoing—dynamic. It demands action. This lends some weight to the cliché that success is a journey rather than a destination. Funny thing about clichés—are they true because they're so common or are they so common because they're true? Meyer believes you must be in the process of achieving. This puts the emphasis on being in the game and not having already achieved the goal. It also implies that just because you've been successful at something doesn't mean you can just sit back and rest on your laurels.

Predetermined. The guy who receives a windfall fortune hardly is a success under this definition. Perhaps that's why so many instant millionaires—like lottery winners—lose their fortunes quickly. Jim Rohn says if you win a million dollars, you'd better become a millionaire quickly so you get to keep it. Well said.

Our goals must be determined in advance. Can you imagine Lee Ioccoca, when asked how he got to the top of Chrysler Corp., saying, "Gosh, I don't know. I didn't really seek it out. I just kept showing up for work every day, they kept promoting me, and here I am."

I don't think so. It takes a plan.

To be a success, we must be consistent and stay focused on our objectives without becoming obsessed by the outcome. It *is* a process. It *is* a journey.

And I think the greatest value comes not from what we attain, but rather by *what we become* in the process.

Our goals must be personal. They must be our own. So often we attempt to accomplish what others want us to achieve. Our goals are things our parents told us to go after. Our goals become things we *should* do instead of labors of love. Trying to achieve someone else's goals causes us to be uninspired and live out of obligation. It leaves us empty and tired.

When we seek out our own objectives—something we feel passionate about—we have an abundance of energy. Our spirit soars and we, as well as those around us, experience more joy. We're in sync with our lives. We feel successful. And we are.

Goals must also be worthwhile. Worthwhile to whom? Worthwhile to you. You get to decide. It's your life. If your aim in life is to study and contemplate the great spiritual mysteries of the universe, that's great. If it's to be the first woman on Mars, then more power to you. As long as your goals are in keeping with your values and don't hurt anybody, you'll achieve success.

"Success is simply a matter of luck. Ask any failure."

—Earl Wilson

"A successful day: to learn something new; to laugh at least 10 times; to lift someone up; to make progress on a worthy goal; to practice peace and patience; to do something nice for yourself and another; to appreciate and be grateful for all your blessings."

—Michael Angier

21. Is that the Best You Can Do?

On a weekend trip a few years ago, my wife and I stayed overnight in southern New Hampshire. As we looked for a place to stay, I remembered a very nice hotel from when I had attended a conference a few years back.

I expected the rooms would be nearly $200, which was more than we wanted to spend. However, I figured it didn't cost anything to look, and it being a weekend, perhaps they had some kind of package or special rate.

When I walked up to the desk, I asked if there was availability for the night. The very pleasant, very friendly desk clerk assured me there was. I mentioned I had been to the hotel before and liked it. I explained that my wife and I were here on a quick trip and would like to stay, if the price was right. Did they have a weekend rate? He said they did and quoted me $110 dollars for a room that went for $175 during the week.

That seemed like a good deal, and I told him so. I then asked him a very important question. I asked him if that was the very best he could do. He hesitated a moment and then asked me to wait. He looked at a couple things on his desk, went back to the room behind the counter and in only a few seconds emerged to tell me that because they weren't very busy this weekend, he could reduce it to $80. I thanked him, and we were shown to our room.

Eighty dollars is about what we would have paid somewhere else, but instead we were staying in a four-star hotel. What a difference. By the way, breakfast was included with the room. It was delicious.

When I bought a car that summer, I also saved money by posing the question. The asking price of the vehicle was far less than it was worth. I know, because when I paid the sales tax on it to the state, I had to pay it on the book value rather than the actual selling price. After looking at several other comparable cars, I went back to the owner and asked a few more questions about the car. Even though I was fully prepared to meet his price, I decided to at least try for a better one. I asked if he would take 10% less than what he was asking. He thought only for a second and then said, "Sure."

By simply asking the question, I saved a bundle. I don't know what your hourly rate is, but mine doesn't come close to what I earned per minute—actually per second—of negotiation in the two examples above.

Am I bragging here? Maybe just a little. But like one guy said, "If it's true, it ain't bragging." I share this with you to help you see the ease and the power of asking the question.

In practically any transaction, simply ask, "Is that the very best you can do?" Ask it with sincerity, ask it in a friendly manner, and you'll get positive results. After all, the worst that can happen is they'll say, "Yes, that's the very best we can do." From there, you can decide for yourself what *you* want to do.

"You don't get what you deserve. You get what you negotiate." Try it. It works.

"The ability to deal with people is as purchasable a commodity as sugar or coffee, and I will pay more for that ability than for any other under the sun."

—Barry Neil Kaufman

"To solve any problem, here are three questions to ask yourself: First, what could I do? Second, what could I read? And third, who could I ask?"

—Jim Rohn

"You can't ask for what you want unless you know what it is. A lot of people don't know what they want or they want much less than they deserve. First you have figure out what you want. Second, you have to decide that you deserve it. Third, you have to believe you can get it. And, fourth, you have to have the guts to ask for it."

—Barbara De Angelis

22. Your Unique Selling Proposition

Your USP (Unique Selling Proposition)—whether for yourself or your business—is a critical part of your marketing success. How many times have you been at a business or social function when you were asked what you did? How did you answer? Were you able to articulate clearly in just a sentence or two what you did and explain it in a way that evoked genuine interest?

Certainly you've asked someone else what they did. And sometimes you probably wished you hadn't because the response was either long, unintelligible, dull or all three.

The ideal is to be able to tell someone who you are, what you do and what's special about that (translated how it might benefit them or someone else) in less than 90 seconds. Hopefully you're excited about what you do, so be sure to let this enthusiasm come across. If you've done it well, the response should be, "No kidding, tell me more."

Your USP should answer the following questions:

- What do you do? Who are you?
- What are the primary benefits to your service/product?
- How do you provide those benefits?
- Why would someone want to do business with you?

If you were to ask me SuccessNet's USP today, I'd say, "We save people time and money by keeping them informed, inspired and directed toward their personal and professional best. We publish ideas and information, provide support and secure product and service discounts for our members. SuccessNet strives to make the navigation of change and uncertainty not only easier, but more fun!"

I'm not yet satisfied with this description. Perhaps I'll never be quite satisfied with it and that's probably good. Just like I'm never satisfied with what we do and how we do it. It's called CANI—Constant And Never-ending Improvement.

How about you? Do you have a USP? Are you satisfied with it?

———⊶∰∻———

"In the factory we make cosmetics; in the store we sell hope."

—Charles Revlon

23. Are You a "Can-Do" Person?

Sad but true. When it comes to the people who can be counted upon to get a job done—correctly and on time—the numbers are few. In my experience, out of a hundred people, the number of get-it-done people are in the single digits.

The good news is if you resolve to become one of these people, you'll easily stand out from the crowd.

Of course there are large numbers of people who manage to hold onto their job simply by doing their job. But I'm talking about working unsupervised. I'm talking about taking initiative—setting a goal or taking on a project—and sticking with it until it's accomplished.

The vast majority of people can show up for a job they dislike but can't seem to set and achieve goals on their own.

And that's what separates the winners from the spectators.

I have a plaque that reads, "There are three kinds of people: those who make it happen, those who watch it happen and those who wonder *what* happened."

In terms of getting it done, I think there are *four* kinds of people:

1. Those who never start.
2. Those who start but give up too quickly.
3. Those who start, work hard and hang in there, but aren't flexible enough with their strategies to complete the project.
4. Those few who start and continue to persist with a willingness to change tactics in order to get it done.

Determine to be one of the few who do instead of the many who don't. Be your word. Do what you resolve to do—every time.

In doing so, you'll develop a habit of completion. You will earn a reputation for being someone who can be counted upon to "get it done."

Daily Action Plan in PDF (Acrobat) format
www.SuccessNet.org/files/DailyActionPlan.pdf

24. The Art of Inspiration

What exactly is inspiration? We often talk about being inspired—inspired to do something, a feeling of inspiration: "I felt inspired." We speak about inspiring people: "She's an inspiring speaker."

The word inspire comes from the word spirit, the Latin spîritus, meaning breath, which was derived from the verb spîrâre 'breathe'. In the Augustan period, it gradually began to take over as the word for soul.

For me, inspiration is something that touches me deep within my soul. I feel it. It's a connection with something bigger than myself. And I like it. Most people do.

Is it possible to be inspired all the time—to stay in touch with something higher than ourselves, to be motivated, enthusiastic—connected? I believe it is.

Inspiring People

An important key to being inspired is to associate with people who are inspiring. They're the kind of people you just feel better being around. You feel more stimulated—more alive. An inspiring person is someone who helps us see and believe in our highest good—someone who helps draw out the very best that's within us.

Conversely, we also want to stay away from people who bring us down.

An inspirational person empowers us to stay motivated and excited about our dreams. They're someone with a vision for a better world. They challenge us to dig deep and encourage us through the tough times.

Inspiring people are good role models. They model excellence and give us something to which to aspire. They share themselves. They're authentic.

Stimulating Ideas and Reminders

In addition to people, good books, tapes and movies can provide impetus for our inspiration. They stimulate our thinking. What we read isn't as important as what the reading causes us to think. We feed our bodies every day—hopefully with good fuel. We need to feed our minds every day as well. Anything that reminds us of who we are and what we're capable of becoming is a valuable tool indeed.

Staying focused on our dreams and our commitment to them is key to staying inspired. Affirmations can be very helpful here.

Music

Music can touch us at a vibratory level in ways that can stimulate and tap the imagination. Music can get us out of our head and more into our heart. Find the music that moves your soul and play it—often.

Our Environment

Where we live, work and play can have a significant influence upon our level of inspiration. The visual, auditory, kinesthetic and even olfactory effect of our surroundings can dramatically impact our ability to operate at our best. It's hard to be inspired when our personal environment is depressing. Clean up and spruce up your personal space and see what a difference it makes.

Solitude

Time alone is critical to tapping into our divinity. Most of us are human doings instead of human beings. Too much emphasis is placed on doing things and not enough on pondering the metaphysical mustiness—to tapping into divine ideas.

It matters not what you call it—meditation, prayer or solitude—communing with our Higher Power is essential to bringing out our full potential.

I wish for you to realize your full and divine potential. I wish for you to live a life of excellence—a life of excitement and joy. I wish for you to be inspired and inspiring.

"If you don't have that inspired enthusiasm which is contagious, whatever you do have is also contagious."

—unknown

"Cease trying to work everything out with your mind. It will get you nowhere. Live by intuition and inspiration, and let your whole life be a revelation."

—Eileen Caddy

25. The Trouble with Sam

"The essential conditions of everything you do must be choice, love, passion."

—Nadia Boulanger

I have a friend (let's call him Sam), who has more potential than most people I know. Sam is well-educated, smart, interesting to talk to and has good people skills. He's one of those people who looks good, smells good—and he's broke.

And I don't mean just financially. His spirit is broken. He's physically overdrawn and emotionally bankrupt.

Sam has read lots of success literature. He has a good grasp of the principles of success. Most people would say he has a good attitude, but they, like me, are somewhat baffled by his less-than-stellar performance.

Sam wants desperately to succeed. He's been successful before. He can do it again. But will he?

So what's Sam's problem? I don't know him well enough to know all the reasons he stays stuck, but I have some observations.

Sam has two major challenges: 1) He doesn't love what he's doing, and 2) he doesn't consistently do the things he knows he must in order to succeed.

Like many people today, Sam wants to make it big. As we see people in their twenties becoming millionaires through stock options and IPOs, it's easy to feel like we've missed—or are *missing*—the boat.

Sam feels a need to remain in his chosen profession because it's what he knows and where he thinks the big bucks can be made. But money won't make him successful. He needs to become successful on the inside before it happens on the outside.

If Sam loved what he did, and it wasn't turning out all that profitable, he could continue to look for ways to make it work. But since it's not working, and he doesn't even like doing it, it seems to me the Universe is telling him loud and clear to make a different career choice.

Like the rabbit in *The Tortoise and the Hare*, Sam works in spurts. He burns out, gets sidetracked and loses momentum. And every time he does, he feels like a failure. His self-esteem plummets and he feels guilty for not doing what he set out to do. Each time this happens, it becomes harder and harder to get started again.

The Hyde School has a philosophy which I support. They don't believe you can get kids to do great things by helping them feel better about themselves. They believe you get kids to feel good about themselves by getting them to do great things. And it works.

I firmly believe that our life works in direct proportion to how well-synched we are to our true purpose—our unique contribution to the world.

When we're engaged in something joyful, it doesn't seem like work, and the results can be magical. As John Ruskin wrote, "When love and skill work together, expect a masterpiece."

Sam didn't arrive at where he is overnight, and he may not turn it around quickly either. There will undoubtedly be major break-throughs and blinding flashes of the obvious, but he needs to stay the course in order to have this happen.

We all need to run (or walk) the race like the tortoise, but also make sure we're in the right race. Clarity of purpose and consistent investments of time and effort toward that purpose will always win.

 Find something you're excited about, set some reasonable goals and take the steps to achieve them. As you succeed in small matters, your confidence and self-worth will climb. From there, you can set some bigger goals and create a bigger game—a game worth playing.

By doing something you love, you'll *enjoy* the price of success instead of *paying* the price of success. Your health will improve, your net worth will go up right along with your self-respect, and you'll affect all those around you in a positive way.

"If a man loves the labor of his trade apart from any question of success or fame, the Gods have called him."

—Robert Louis Stevenson

"Work is love made visible. And when you work with love you bind yourself to yourself, and to one another and to God."

—Kahlil Gibran

26.   What the Coach Meant by "Being Perfect"

"Strong lives are motivated by dynamic purposes."

—Kenneth Hildebrand

I recently watched a movie named "Friday Night Lights." It's based on a book by H. G. Bissinger that chronicles head coach Gary Gaines (played by Billy Bob Thornton) and his winning high school football team (the Panthers) from a small town in Texas.

Now, for those of you who don't live in the southern part of the United States, you have to understand that most southern folks take football very, *very* seriously.

One could say there are two religions in the Bible Belt—Christianity and football. And some would say there's no difference between them. Everything is big in Texas and football is *huge*.

The movie follows the coach and his team in their quest of a state championship. Throughout the season, the coach urges his players to "be perfect."

There's a lot of pressure on the Panthers—from parents, from the town fathers, the coaches and from the players themselves. It seems like winning is everything—especially the Texas state championship.

The most inspiring part of the movie for me was the half-time speech Coach Gaines gives his squad in the locker room at the state championship. The Panthers are behind, and they must turn the tide in the second half in order to win.

Only a couple of these players will ever suit up for another football game again. It's an experience they'll remember for the rest of their lives. The competition is tough, and they are far behind.

As if he needed to, Coach Gaines reminds them about all of this. And then he tells them what he means by "being perfect."

I may not have it exactly the way he said it, but I think I have the essence of his inspiring speech:

> *"I want you to know what I mean by being perfect. It's not about that scoreboard out there. It's not about winning. It's about you and your relationship with yourself, with your family and with your friends.*

> *It's about being able to look your family and friends in the eye, knowing that you didn't let them down—because you told them the truth—that you did everything you possibly could out there. There wasn't one more thing you could have done.*
>
> *Being perfect is living as best you can—with clear eyes, with love in your heart, with joy in your heart. And it lasts forever. Can you live in that manner? If you can, gentlemen—then you're perfect."*

Whether we're playing a game, building a business or raising a family, we would do well to go after all our goals and dreams with that kind of heart—with that kind of commitment.

 If you're not playing full out, either choose something that's more worthy of your best efforts or recommit to what you're doing. You may want to rate yourself on the go-for-it-scale in each of your endeavors. Whatever you do, resolve to do your best. And "be perfect."

"If you appreciate what you already have, you'll find yourself having even more to appreciate."

"Success is the accumulation of successful days."

—Michael Angier

"Be willing to be uncomfortable. Be comfortable being uncomfortable. It may get tough, but it's a small price to pay for living a dream."

—Peter McWilliams

"It may be those who do most, dream most."

—Stephen Leacock

27. The Power of Acknowledgement

In the early days of January 2005, I had the honor and privilege of attending two semi-formal ceremonies. First was the swearing-in of Vermont's Lieutenant Governor in the well of the state senate. The second was the Governor's Inaugural Ball at our country's oldest military academy, Norwich University.

I'm not all that big on pomp and pageantry, but I was glad to attend and very much enjoyed myself. In doing so, I was reminded of the importance of acknowledging and honoring people.

It was during the Lieutenant Governor's inauguration speech that I was struck with just how powerful acknowledgement truly is.

Lieutenant Governor Brian Dubie had just taken the oath of office for his second term, and he was addressing the Vermont Senate, a number of friends, family and a few dignitaries.

Lieutenant Governor Dubie is a Colonel in the Vermont Air Force Reserve and has a good number of his family in the military. There were over 20 people in uniform with us in the Senate Chamber.

One of those who was asked to stand and be recognized was my father J. Francis Angier. Lt. Governor Dubie talked about how my father served our country and our state when he was a B-17 bomber pilot during WWII, how he was shot down and how he had been a POW held by the Germans until the end of the war. He even went so far as to hold up a copy of my father's book *Ready or Not!*, calling it "a great book."

I was proud, my father was a tad bit embarrassed, and we were both a little surprised.

The acknowledgement and tribute paid to my father and a host of others during Brian's speech really impressed me. Most of his speech was spent recognizing and honoring people. He spoke only a little about his own accomplishments—of which there are many— and his plans for the future.

Our gracious Lt. Governor obviously understands the value and inspiration that comes from giving public recognition to the help someone has given or the work someone has done. Everyone who heard Brian that snowy morning was reminded of the selfless acts of many people. He inspired us all by honoring dozens of people who have made all our lives better.

Two days later, at the Governor's Inaugural Ball, both Lt. Governor Brian Dubie and Governor Jim Douglas toasted our guardsmen deployed around the world and many others who serve our country and our community in different capacities.

In my opinion, they honored themselves, by honoring others—and so can—and should—we.

 Look for every opportunity to publicly acknowledge others for their good deeds. Tell people about the goodness and kindness of others. Look for the examples of what's good in the world—in small ways and big—and point it out for everyone to see.

"No one who achieves success does so without acknowledging the help of others. The wise and confident acknowledge this help with gratitude."

—Alfred North Whitehead

"Great people are those who make others feel that they, too, can become great."

—Mark Twain

28. But What About When it's *Not* a Great Day?

"Peter" from Oklahoma, wrote to me with a question about an article I had written on making every day a great day.

It seems that on a recent flight, his luggage was lost, and it took 36 hours to recover it. The airline was somewhat apologetic but unwilling to provide any compensation—not even a few extra miles on their frequent flyer program.

Peter said, "I'm having trouble finding a way to see a positive side to having the airline lose my luggage. Yeah, I can look at it positively by accepting poor service, but what does it teach me and the company? Put up with whatever corporations will give you and love it? So how do you turn that into a good day?"

It's a good question. And I may not be able to answer it to his—or your—satisfaction.

Most of us have been in Peter's position. We've all been inconvenienced and frustrated when it wasn't remedied to our satisfaction.

There's some advice from the Bible that says, "Give thanks in all things." Notice it doesn't say, *for* all things. We don't have to be grateful *for* everything that happens. But our experience is mostly dependent upon our point of view.

There might be some positive aspects to our luggage being lost, but not likely. It's usually a bummer.

But we can be grateful *in* all things. If our luggage truly does not arrive at its intended destination at the appropriate time, there's nothing we can do about it. It's done.

What we *can* do something about is how we respond. It's a fact the luggage isn't there. And it's undoubtedly true it will be unhandy to be without it. But from that point on, what meaning we assign to the experience and the actions we take or don't take is up to us.

If we choose to indulge our anger at the airline (for this and all previous transgressions), we manufacture harmful chemicals in our body that can only make things worse. We reduce our resourcefullness and often become unpleasant to be around.

If there's something we can do about the situation, we should do it. If not, we need to accept what is and make the best of it.

It's not always easy, but that's how we keep this and every day from being a bad day.

If our focus is on what's wrong, that's what will grow. If our focus is on what's right and/or what can be done, then that will increase. There are many things outside our control, but there are also many things we *do* have control over.

A little over a hundred years ago, a trip across the country took many months, and if more than half the travelers made it through alive, it was considered a successful trip. Today, people get upset if their flight is delayed a couple of hours or their luggage is lost.

I'm not trying to make light of Peter's situation. Nor am I making excuses for the airline not doing a better job or making things right when they messed up. But in the whole scheme of things, it really is small stuff. It's we who make these things into big things.

Lost luggage is nothing compared to finding out your wife or husband has been diagnosed with cancer. It's nothing compared to finding two uniformed officers at your door with news your son or daughter has been killed in action. We have to put things in perspective.

 There are easy days and there are hard days. You will have good days and bad. And when you maintain your perspective, when you do your best with what you have, when you overcome the tendency to blame and when you're able to remain calm when most others are freaking out, *that's* a great day.

"He who is of calm and happy nature will hardly feel the pressure of age, but to him who is of an opposite disposition youth and age are equally a burden."

—Plato

29. Tips for Being a Better Writer

Whether you're writing a memo, a letter, an article or a full-length novel, there are a few basic rules to keep in mind to help your message be better understood and accepted.

1. **Never Be Boring**
   Your reader will forgive almost anything except you being boring. They don't have to agree with you, but they should at least be intrigued. Don't be afraid to be "edgy." Look at every sentence and ask yourself, "Why will they care about this?"

2. **Write in Short Sentences**
   The reader shouldn't have to work hard to understand what you're saying. If they have to go back over a sentence because of poor structure, it's not their fault; it's yours. Read what you've written aloud or have someone else read it aloud to look for sentences that are too long or convoluted.

3. **Write *to* the Reader**
   Use "you" often. Look for ways to eliminate or reduce "I" and "me." Present tense, second person is always best. It feels more to the reader like you're talking to *them*.

4. **Go Active**
   Use active verbs as much as possible. They're more engaging. They move the reader along and take fewer words to get your message across. "John loves Mary" is much more powerful than "Mary is loved by John."

5. **Keep it Simple**
   The front page of *The Wall Street Journal* and all of *USA Today* is written for the eighth-grade reading level. People aren't interested in things they don't understand. Make your points quickly and succinctly.

6. **Tell Stories**
   Facts tell and stories sell. The best writers and speakers of the world have always been good story tellers. Your own stories are the best. What you're sharing is wisdom from your point of view and stories can illustrate this better than anything else.

7. **Know Your Subject**
   Write on things on which you've earned the right to write. Know 100 times more about your subject than you write about, but don't write about all of it. The more you know, the more confidence—and credibility—you'll have.

8. **WIFM**

This is the radio station everyone listens to. The call letters stand for What's in It For Me. People want to know what they'll get out of what you're writing. Appeal to what they want.

9. **Write Like You Talk**

Or at least the way you'd *like* to talk. Too many times, I see people who are good verbal communicators try to put on a different air in their writing. It doesn't work. It's much better to be conversational.

10. **Paint Pictures**

We think in pictures and should write in ways that create these pictures in the mind of the reader. Be descriptive. Use examples. Describe the unfamiliar by using some of the familiar. "Jennifer's first day at her new job reminded her of the freshness and unfamiliarity she experienced on her first day of school."

11. **Sleep On it**

It's a rare individual who can sit down and write something well at the first attempt. Any writing of import should be written and then reviewed later—preferably at least a day later. Some things should be edited several times over an extended period of time.

12. **Write and Read Extensively**

This advice is from Stephen King—a prolific writer. If you want to be a good writer, you have to do two things—read a lot and write a lot.

13. **Break it Down**

Where appropriate, use bullet points. Use them for summaries or outlines. Think about someone who may only start out by scanning your text. Let your bullet points draw the reader in.

A Few Points for Email Writing

14. **Keep your lines 60-65 characters maximum.** A column that's too wide taxes the eyes of the reader and appears overwhelming.

15. **Keep paragraphs to no more than six lines.** Short paragraphs provide white space to the text. They break up the page and make it appear less formidable to the reader. As in music, the space between the notes is as important as the notes themselves.

16. **Don't use all caps.** Capital letters are harder to read than upper and lower case. They also can be perceived as SHOUTING! A little uppercase usage is OK. But using all caps doesn't work and looks amateurish.

30. Ten Ways to Create Breakthroughs

break·through *(brāk' throo') noun, a major achievement or success that permits further progress.*

Breakthroughs are exciting. They're inspiring. They're not business as usual. That's why they're called breakthroughs. Incremental progress is boring. What gets attention, what fires us with enthusiasm, is seeing results that are beyond the ordinary. Here are ten ways to have more breakthroughs, whether it be in your business, your job or your relationships.

1. **Expect Them**
   Too often, we get bogged down in the thick of thin things. We don't expect exciting events to happen, much less make them happen. But when we start to expect major breakthroughs, they start to come about on a regular basis. Not by themselves but through awareness, attention and expectation.

2. **Look for the Breakdowns**
   Breakdowns lead to breakthroughs. It starts by looking for problems that need to be solved in new ways. You find what you're looking for. Declare breakdowns when they occur. Too often, problems get swept under the rug. People want to avoid them. Instead of living in denial, shine a light on what's not working with an eye toward what could be.

3. **Define the Breakdowns**
   A problem clearly stated is a problem half solved. Look for ways to state the problem differently. Simply articulating the problem in a new way can illuminate the solution. Get a different perspective by writing the problem down several different ways.

4. **Live in the Possibility**
   What could happen here? What would be a game worth playing? Don't just go for the obvious—be bold. What will turn this solution into a breakthrough? What would you attempt if you knew you couldn't fail? This is often the toughest part. But to let go of what we *think* is possible and operate in the realm of possibility is when things really start to change.

5. **Make the Commitment**
   Stating what you're planning to accomplish takes courage. Most people want to see the evidence first. They don't want to commit to something unless it's all set up. But when you commit to going for a big goal that appears impossible, you inspire others. Tell people what you intend to accomplish. And don't be bashful.

6. **Enroll Others**

   You don't need to go it alone. People like to be part of something bigger than themselves. They're flattered by someone asking for their opinion or ideas. Put together a team. Keep focused on the intended results, not on what's happened before. Do some brainstorming. And have fun.

7. **Do Your Research**

   Many people try to reinvent the wheel. Often a problem can be solved in a similar way that another problem was solved. Perhaps in a different industry, in a different company, during another era. By reading and studying what others do or have done, you can often relate it to your own situation.

8. **Stay Open to Ideas and Insights**

   Some of the best ideas and inventions have come as flashes of insight—oftentimes when they were least expected. Archimedes was taking a bath. Isaac Newton was taking a snooze under an apple tree. Moodling is the art of doing nothing creatively—expecting ideas to come to us when our minds are at rest. Don't underestimate it.

9. **Declare Breakthroughs**

   Just as important as declaring breakdowns is the declaration of breakthroughs. Announce your achievement to your team, your coworkers, your family—even the press—when you've succeeded. Document it. Your energy flows where your attention goes. Give attention to your breakthroughs.

10. **Celebrate Your Success.**

    You deserve it. Make it fun. Olympic medal winners get their moment in the sun and you deserve nothing less. Mark the event. And ready yourself for "breakthroughs as usual."

31. An Upset is an Opportunity to See the Truth

A few days ago my wife and I found ourselves in a dilemma.

We rarely have arguments, and I wouldn't characterize this as one. It was, however, an upset. Hurt feelings, frustration, misunderstandings and ego all played their negative roles.

We've been together for almost ten years and have worked through many of the challenges of any marriage, including blended families, teenagers, illnesses, money issues and the like. We feel blessed to have a compatible, supportive and loving relationship, but it wasn't just given to us; we worked for it.

So it was a bit surprising for us to find ourselves in the midst of an issue that didn't appear resolvable. We were at a loss to even accurately describe what the issue was.

We know that people rarely fight about what they *think* they're fighting about. Knowing this, we still found ourselves stuck. We both expressed our inadequacy to find a way through the quagmire, while at the same time realizing this issue was keeping us from our steadfast commitment to constantly improve our marriage and ourselves.

At several points, we were tempted to chalk it up to a case of Mars versus Venus and two different people having different and conflicting needs and wants.

But we kept talking. We kept asking questions. We applied Steven Covey's principle: "Seek first to understand." It wasn't always easy, but we kept digging.

And then it happened.

Staring us in the face was the beautiful truth. Not the ugly truth. Not the bitter truth—just the truth. It was something that didn't even seem all that related to what we *thought* the issue was. It was something two intelligent, dedicated people had failed to see in almost ten years of living and loving together.

We both felt several pounds lighter. We started breathing easier. Our faces brightened and we felt not just relieved but joyful.

You may want to know what it was, but it doesn't really matter. It's too personal, and it wouldn't really add anything to this story.

The point is, the upset was the catalyst for a breakthrough.

And this is true in all relationships—whether they are intimate, business, social or relationships between countries.

What's key is having trust in the other party, having some shared values and having a commitment to seeing things through.

With these things as the foundation, a relationship can withstand and even grow through any controversy that arises. What appear as breakdowns can lead to breakthroughs.

"Sometimes only a change of viewpoint is needed to convert a tiresome duty into an interesting opportunity."

—Alberta Flanders

"Opportunity is missed by most people because it comes dressed in overalls and looks like work."

—Thomas Alva Edison

"I am never upset for the reason I think."

—A Course in Miracles

"Seek first to understand and then to be understood."

—Stephen Covey

32. Making Things Work Better Every Day with S-O-D-A

We all need a certain amount of routine in our lives. It provides us with comfort and familiarity from which we can do our job. But when our routine becomes mundane and monotonous, it's hard to be creative and do our best.

I'm hardly ever bored—too many interesting and challenging things to do, I guess. But I do sometimes find myself doing repetitious work that I don't like.

When I'm doing anything that feels tedious, I lose interest quickly. I feel like a machine, and my creativity suffers. I'm willing to do what's necessary to get the job done, but I always want to find a better, faster, easier or more productive way to accomplish things.

The challenge is to be efficient *and* effective. We want to do things with efficiency and expediency, but we also need to be doing the things that matter most—to be *effective.*

There are all kinds of techniques to help us manage our tasks and the events in our lives. I have a little acrostic that's worked really well for me.

I call it SODA. It stands for Simplify, Automate, Delegate or Organize. I try to do something in at least one of these areas each day. It keeps me focused on ways to make my work, my business and my household work better.

> **S**implify
> **O**rganize
> **D**elegate
> **A**utomate

At the beginning of each day, I strive to simplify something, organize something, delegate (outsource) or automate or systemize something I'm doing.

At the end of the day, I review what I've done, how I did it and look for ways to make my tasks less tedious. In doing so, I'm constantly making improvements and having more fun in the process. It keeps me energized and motivated. It helps me to be more creative and innovative. It's also profitable.

 Give it a try. Post the SODA acrostic over your desk and apply it for 30 days. I'm sure you'll see a difference.

33. Your Most Precious Asset

Albert Einstein was once asked to explain, in layman's terms, his Theory of Relativity. He replied this way. "If you sit with a beautiful woman, two hours seem like two minutes. If you sit on a hot stove, two minutes seem like two hours. That's relativity."

That might be an oversimplification, but it makes a point. What we do and how we feel about what we do is critical to our perception of time. And time *is* our most valuable asset. What would you value any more than time? Certainly not material possessions.

For many people, time seems to be treated as if it were in never-ending supply. It's rare I find someone who has a profound regard for this building block of life.

Most everyone you know is probably busy. But the question is, "busy with what?" Are we investing our time or just spending it?

How is it some people seem to get so much done while others accomplish so little? Why are there some times when we're able to be highly productive and other times when we're not?

There are no easy answers.

We all have the same amount of time, and if you've read this far, you probably want to maximize the time you have. Maximize it to do the things you want to do with the greatest enjoyment and the most productivity.

This issue is very much "up" for me. I'm busier than I've ever been. I love what I do (at least most of it). There just doesn't seem to be enough hours in the day to do all the things I want to do. And, of course, there aren't. It's true we can do anything we want to do; we just can't do *everything* we want to do.

So what's the answer? Well, I have good news and bad news. The bad news is we can't manage time. The good news is we can manage tasks and projects.

It's a skill that can be learned by anyone, but we have to be willing to invest the time (there it is again) to learn how to make excellent use of this precious commodity. It's something that will reward us for the rest of our lives—whether we have 1 year or 100.

How to Get Control of Time and Your Life, by Alan Laikin.
www.SuccessNet.org/books/laikin-time.htm

34. How to Solve Problems in Your Sleep

Employing the Science of Universal Delegation

Would you like to utilize a strategy that's been used for thousands of years by most of the world's great minds? Inventors, writers, artists, scientists and philosophers have employed this technique to solve problems and create works of art. This is a simple but almost magical method for gaining access to Universal Wisdom.

You've probably already used it yourself either intentionally or unintentionally. I've had great success with the process, and must admit that I don't employ it as often as I should. I forget about how powerful, effective and easy it is. Perhaps we've just been programmed to believe that solving difficult problems needs to involve struggle and effort.

Just what is this magical, mystical process? It's simply turning a problem or question over to our subconscious (some say super-conscious) mind and trusting enough to await the result. I call it "Universal Delegation"—charging the Universe with a problem or question (big or small).

By tasking your subconscious to provide you with solutions or answers to your request, you're tapping into a whole realm of memory and wisdom that's difficult to reach when we're awake. I recognize that what I'm sharing may have a fairly high "woo-woo" factor. And it *does* involve a certain degree of trust in the process in order for it to be successful.

Let's take a practical example that can explain at least a part of how this all works. Have you ever tried to think of someone's name but couldn't? Try as hard as you might, you just couldn't come up with it. Finally, after having given up on your memory scan—sometime when you weren't even thinking about it, the name came to you in a flash. Instead of forcing the data from your memory banks, your unconscious mind went about it with seemingly no effort on your part. Much the same thing happens using Universal Delegation. And it's even more powerful.

Charles Kettering said that a "problem clearly stated is a problem half-solved." I believe that. Some of the success of this practice may come just from becoming clear about the problem and asking specifically for what we want. Try it. You have nothing to lose and everything to gain.

Before going to sleep, charge your unconscious to give you what you want. Be very clear about what you're requesting. Your subconscious doesn't do well with generalities. It likes specifics. The mere process of articulating exactly what you want sets the process in motion.

Then, let it go. Think about it no more. This is not an exercise in having your problem roll around in your head and prevent you from sleeping. Think about some other pleasant and joyful thing as you fall asleep.

For instance: Let's say you're launching a new project and you're unclear about the best way to proceed. Perhaps you don't have all the information you need. Ask your sleeping mind for five (be specific) elegant and innovative strategies to complete the project.

And expect answers. Think of it as asking the wisest and most powerful being in the world for the solution(s). In a way, you're doing just that. Believe that something greater than yourself is providing the wisdom for you.

Don't worry if you don't get it right away—especially when you're just starting to utilize this process. Just keep asking and be patient. The ideas will come—sometimes immediately upon awakening, sometimes in the shower, sometimes while jogging. Just be open to the insight and wisdom your unconscious will offer up. For indeed it will.

"Any thought that is passed on to the subconscious often enough and convincingly enough is finally accepted."

—Robert Collier

"No problem can be solved from the same level of consciousness that created it."

—Albert Einstein

35. What Worked, What Didn't, What's Next?

One of the common denominators of successful people is their ability to persevere when things don't go as planned. Effective people don't allow themselves to get bogged down in feelings that don't serve their purpose.

On the other hand, ineffective, unsuccessful people allow their emotions to rule rather than their rational and objective nature. They lament what happened or what didn't and become victims rather than masters of their circumstances.

We all have disappointments. We all suffer setbacks. If we're going to attempt anything worthwhile, we're going to experience failure. The mature—and ultimately successful—person sees failure as part of success. When one method fails, they try again with a new one. Sometimes it takes many attempts.

In my coaching/consulting work, I see all too often the tendency to fix blame instead of fix problems. Rather than looking at challenges rationally and objectively, emotions are allowed to dictate the process.

They're unable to make corrections without invalidation. Something goes wrong and they want to blame. Profit isn't reached fast enough and someone needs to be fired. There's never a shortage of people or things on which to blame the failure.

I suggest a different approach. It's a process I call, "What Worked, What Didn't, What's Next?"

This practice works whether you're dealing with a business, a relationship, a project or your life. The key is to evaluate often, objectively and then to move on.

And the more often and impartially you measure and evaluate, the better it works. It's just feedback—and feedback is neither positive nor negative. It's simply information. I call feedback the "Breakfast of Champions." Looking at what happened with a healthy degree of detachment allows us to make better decisions.

What Worked?
What actions moved us toward our objective? What's worth repeating? What felt good? What created excellence?

Acknowledge your successes. Celebrate! Praise your own as well as the efforts of others.

When you focus on what worked, you begin with positive energy. And you create momentum toward solutions.

What Didn't?

OK, where did we screw up? What created the mistake? Not *who* dropped the ball, but when, where and how did we drop it? How can we avoid it next time?

It's rarely *people* who mess up but rather systems that don't adequately support them. Most people mean well and try their best. The focus should be on how to better support one another to reduce errors and increase quality.

There are many ways to accomplish what you desire. Often, in finding *new* ways, we create things we never would have if the first or second effort had succeeded.

Acknowledge the mistakes, make new plans and devise new strategies.

What's Next?

Regardless of how well or how badly things went, *it's history.* Nothing is going to change the past. Being upset about it, feeling guilty, placing blame or even resting too long on our laurels will cause us to lose headway.

One might be wise to use the U.S. Marine Corps acronym, FIDO— *Forget It, Drive On.* But I would add one more piece: learn from the experience.

After you analyze what happened, the question should be, "What's next?" This takes the focus off from what's happened and places it on where we're going and what needs doing.

You can quickly go through this process alone or with a group. It can take a few moments or several hours, depending on the complexity of the project.

The key is to do it with impartiality and objectivity. Mistakes, corrections and new attempts are merely part of successful ventures. They don't mean anything; they're simply opportunities to create excellence.

36. How to Help Your Company Become a World Class Company

Most people think real change in an organization occurs as a result of top-level leadership. This isn't always the case.

Oftentimes, it's someone within the rank and file who stands up and challenges the status quo. Remember the old adage, "If the people will lead, the leaders will follow."

Years ago, I was the sales manager for a company with about 30 employees. The business was struggling, and a management consultant had been called in to try and get things back on track.

In one of my meetings with the consultant, I told him about some of the things that were going on that I didn't agree with. I explained that even though we were all encouraged to be open and honest, I feared that what I had to say might cost me my job.

His response was something I won't forget. He asked me if I really wanted to work for a company that said one thing and did another. He showed me that I really didn't have anything to lose.

It was time to walk my talk. I could no longer hide behind the fear of losing my job. I had to speak my truth. I did, and I didn't get fired. And even if I had been fired, it would have been worth it.

Anyone can be the catalyst for change. Sometimes all it takes is a question. Sometimes it requires a brave person pointing to the dusty mission statement hanging on the wall and saying, "Does this reflect our purpose?" or "Is this consistent with our core values?"

Those responsible for the Enron and WorldCom scandals did not do their greedy deeds in a vacuum. Others knew something wasn't right, and yet they remained silent. At the very least, we all have a responsibility to report illegal activity. We also should work toward making our company a world class company.

Yes, it's true that it's risky. It takes courage. But like that consultant said to me, what do you really have to lose? Better to shake things up a bit than remain silent. It's easier to find another job with a company more in tune with your values than to treat an ulcer or high blood pressure. Besides, it's the right thing to do.

Sometimes leadership becomes enlightened by blinding flashes of the obvious illuminated by those in the trenches. And if management can't handle the truth, it's time to seek out new management.

My personal belief is whether you work for—or own—a company, you want it to be something you're proud of. You want the time and energy you invest in your career to be worthy of the best that's within you. You want it to make a difference.

Average isn't good enough. You want to look back on your contribution with pride. Just putting in your time and collecting a paycheck may work for some people, but it shouldn't be sufficient for you. Stand up for excellence. Help your company become a world class company.

 You can challenge with respect. You can question without being insubordinate. In so many instances, I've found that when just one person stands up for what's right, others step forward as well. A leader doesn't have to be elected or appointed. A leader is often someone who cares enough to speak what's in the hearts and minds of others.

 To get SuccessNet's free report 'The Ten Pillars of a World Class Business', send an email to wcb@successnet.org

For full details on World Class Business, go to www.WorldClassBusiness.com

"Excellence can be obtained if you:
        ...care more than others think is wise;
        ...risk more than others think is safe;
        ...dream more than others think is practical;
        ...expect more than others think is possible."

—unknown

"Business is a lot like playing tennis; if you serve well, you'll usually end up winning."

—Michael Angier

37. What Do You Value Most?

Abraham Mazlow defined self-actualization as, "a bringing together of what I do and what I really value."

If you want to create more value in the world and become more valuable in the marketplace, then you'll want to define, embody and live your core values.

No matter how old (or young) you are, you have values that are important to you. You may not be able to articulate what they are right now, but you have them nonetheless.

In fact, our lives are a result of the choices we've made or neglected to make around these values. Everything we do and everything we choose *not* to do is based—or at least *should* be based—upon our hierarchy of values.

The problem is, few of us have a good handle on what these values are. As a result, we may very well find ourselves with possessions, jobs and relationships that are unfulfilling and sometimes even painful.

When we're clear on what we want, clear on our core values—on who we are and what we stand for—there's no stopping us. The decisions we make become easier, our work becomes more interesting.

We have more energy and it takes a lot more to discourage us. Our successes are sweeter and our defeats easier to bear. We arrive at our accomplishments with a clear conscience and with more pride and satisfaction.

By living our values, we experience fulfillment. We know we're in the process of achieving what's important to us, and we do it in a way that makes us feel good about ourselves. Our self-esteem goes up and our attitude improves with it. We are truly successful in every sense of the word.

Regardless of whether I'm working with individuals or organizations, I find the biggest problem or roadblock to their success is lack of clarity and focus. They're often busy doing the wrong things. They want me to help them climb a ladder that's often leaning against the wrong wall. What they really need is a clear sense of vision and a foundation of core values that can support that vision. The rest really isn't all that hard.

It's not always fun, easy or exciting to sort through the many values one might hold near and dear and to find the five on which we want to build our life. It takes hard work. It takes thinking. It requires being open to our inner voice.

But the payoff is substantial. It may be the most important thing you ever do. It will dramatically and permanently impact the rest of your life. Big investment—big return. Small investment—small return.

People who have it together are people who are clear on their values—they know what they stand for. They're not perfect, but they *are* congruent. They know, and others know, what's important to them.

Are you willing to invest some time in your most important asset? Is your life worth your best effort? Do you want to be efficient and effective with your time? Do you want your family to experience the best of you? Do you want to live an exceptional life?

If you can say yes to these questions, then begin today to discover your values. Your future depends on it.

 Start by asking yourself a few questions. Do some journaling about what comes up. What are my most important values? Why are they important? What am I willing to fight for? What do I stand for?

 SuccessNet has an eCourse on discovering, articulating and living your core values. In taking "Your Core Values," you'll be able to lay the foundation for a fulfilling and rewarding life—one based on *your* values.
www.YourCoreValues.com

38. It's a Matter of Manners

Something happened to me recently that stood out as an uncommon event.

It happened when I was greeting a friend as he brought his boat into our marina. As I was standing on the dock, he introduced me to 'Karen' and her son 'Hunter'. This seven-year-old bounded out of the boat and walked the length of the dock toward me. He extended his hand, looked me in the eye and said, "How do you do?"

The good manners he demonstrated by these simple actions were impressive—not just because he is so young, but because they are so rare.

I'm not a stickler for proper etiquette. I'm talking about just plain good manners—about being polite.

We get phone calls at our home from teenagers, as well as adults, who don't introduce themselves or say "hello" to the person answering the phone. They just say, "Is ____ there?" And these are people who know us.

We've even been to showers and weddings where we never received a thank you card for the gifts given.

I'm sure you have your own list of boorish behaviors that irritate you.

Good manners are never out of style. And most of them are common sense—please, thank you, you're welcome and good day go a long way toward better human relations. A good handshake is an important social skill.

What does this have to do with success and personal development? Plenty.

People judge us by our actions. To get along in our culture, we need to show respect and be courteous. It's easy to turn people off by less-than-respectful behavior. On the other hand, it's easy to stand out by exercising even a modicum of good manners.

Young Hunter impressed me and made his mother proud by showing good manners. It made me think about how important and yet how lacking good manners are in our society.

Good manners don't cost anything to exercise, but the lack of them may be costing us more than we know.

 Look at your own manners and how you might improve them. You don't need to be stuffy. You just need to look for ways you can be more kind, considerate and polite. It's important to be a good example. Kids watch much more closely than they listen.

Talking to your kids and others you influence about the importance of good manners. Ask people what they observe that bothers them. Get a conversation going and put some focus on decorum.

"Politeness is to human nature what warmth is to wax."

—Arthur Schopenhauer

"Manners are a sensitive awareness of the feelings of others. If you have that awareness, you have good manners, no matter what fork you use."

—Emily Post

"Good manners will open doors that the best education cannot."

—Clarence Thomas

39. Ten Ways to Foster Innovation

In order to compete effectively, we must look for new and better ways to accomplish our mission. We must find creative methods to delight our customers. And we must find innovative strategies for getting more done with fewer resources.

With things changing as rapidly as they are, doing things the old way won't be profitable for very long. To grow, we must be constantly innovating.

An innovative company attracts and keeps better employees. People want to be part of something creative. It's stimulating and it's fun.

Here are ten things you can do to foster a culture of innovation and creativity.

1. **Live in the possibility.** Stand in the belief that you and your team can find a better way to do anything to which you put your minds. Practice CANI—Constant and Never-Ending Improvement.

2. **Always question what you do and why you do it.** All too often, tasks and projects creep into our processes that are no longer in keeping with our mission and purpose. Make sure everything you do is in alignment and produces the results intended.

3. **Challenge long-held beliefs.** Just because something's always been done a certain way doesn't mean that it's still the best way. As Anthony D'Angelo said, "Just because something is tradition doesn't make it right."

4. **Don't accept the first solution right away.** There are many possible solutions to every problem. Most people go with the first plausible one that comes up, and they miss the value of taking the time to think longer and of finding more effective and elegant answers.

5. **Read.** You can't learn less. The more you know about something, the more you find that you *don't* know. By adding to your knowledge base, you find more and more associ-ations. And making associations is where seemingly magical things happen.

6. **Have fun.** Coming up with ideas on how to do things faster, easier, with fewer resources, really is fun. And things that are fun to do get done more often. Schedule regular brain-storming sessions and practice green-light thinking. Order pizza

for lunch and focus on a problem or process and generate as many ideas as you can.

7. **Get around people in different industries.** By stepping out of your familiar territory, you open the door to new and different viewpoints you can use to your advantage.

8. **Challenge your team to look deeper.** When Henry Ford asked his engineers to design the V-8 engine, they said it couldn't be done. He said it *will* be done—and eventually, they did it.

9. **Make sure you have adequate "moodling" time—time to do nothing.** When we're constantly engaged in *doing* things, we don't provide the fertile ground for ideas to take root.

10. **Charge your subconscious.** Give your mind something to work on while you sleep. Select a problem you want solved, a process you would like improved or a new product you want to create before going to bed. Then forget about it. Tell yourself you want at least three elegant ideas by the next day and then expect to receive them. Trust me, it works.

40. What Are You Tolerating in Your Life?

Making the principle of vacuum work for you

In order to be successful, it's critical we become clear about what we really want and why we want it. And the flip side to that is to also be clear about what we *don't* want.

We all have things in our lives that, at best, don't serve us. Many of these things actually detract from the quality and satisfaction of our lives. What we've found to be helpful is to create a toleration list.

By simply listing the things we don't want, we begin the process of their removal. I'm not advocating we dwell on these things—only that we identify them and begin to eliminate them. I'm a firm believer in keeping our focus on what we want because we tend to find what we're looking for. But we must also discern that which we *don't* want as part of our experience.

Much time and energy is frittered away by small but annoying things: a dent in our car, a window in the house that doesn't shut easily, a towel rack that's bent, a squeaky door, a button missing or a phone with an unpleasant ring. They may not sound like much, but added together, they reduce our creativity, sap our production ability and detract from our enjoyment of everyday living.

Identifying and writing these things down is the genesis of their eradication.

I just looked at a toleration list my wife and I made a few months ago and was surprised to see how many items had been handled— seemingly without effort. One by one we knocked them off because we'd identified them as worthy of elimination. As a result, we have a greater sense of accomplishment and things run more smoothly.

Of course, there are now other things we've added to our list. We've also found that our tolerance level has been elevated. We no longer put up with things we used to accept.

As you get rid of things, you're using the principle of vacuum— making room for what you want by getting rid of what you don't. If your life is filled with things that no longer serve you, there's no room for the things that can.

And there's no need to make these items on our list bad or wrong, either. Handling the things on your toleration list is just another way of taking out the trash.

 Start a list of tolerations. Write down all the things that don't work, don't look good—that you don't like using, looking at or having around. Go through your wardrobe and give away what doesn't work for you anymore—if it ever did. Walk through your house and list things that are broken, shabby or create clutter.

Start your toleration list today, begin to eliminate each item and watch the quality of your life, your creativity and your productivity soar.

"Any time you sincerely want to make a change, the first thing you must do is to raise your standards. When people ask me what really changed my life eight years ago, I tell them that absolutely the most important thin was changing what I demanded of myself. I wrote down all the things I would no longer accept in my life, all the things I would no longer tolerate, and all the things that I aspired to becoming."

—Tony Robbins

"There are those who believe something, and therefore will tolerate nothing; and on the other hand, those who tolerate everything, because they believe nothing."

—Robert Browning

"Happiness happens when you know yourself, your true calling and that you get what you tolerate."

—John G. Agno

41. Ten Ways to Deal with Overwhelm

Lately, many of the people I've been talking with or coaching have been complaining about being overwhelmed. I have to admit I've been wrestling with it, too.

My ideas and my commitments seem to far outpace my time and energy. So here's my advice to you—and to myself—for dealing with overwhelm.

1. **Recognize that overwhelm isn't real.** It's not something that attacks us. It's a feeling we experience based upon a belief there's too much to do and too little time to do it. It's fear—plain and simple. And once we recognize and acknowledge it, we're better equipped to deal with it.

2. **Be grateful.** Just think, the alternative is that you have little to do and you're bored. Appreciate the fact that you have the opportunities and the projects that allow you to contribute to the world.

3. **Accept that you'll never be caught up.** If you're a person of action—someone with goals and aspirations—it's not too likely you'll ever have an empty inbox. The times in which we live and our ability to do meaningful work throughout our lives lead me to believe we'll always have things left to do.

4. **Understand we can only think about one thing at a time.** We may be able to multi-task, and we may be able to switch our thoughts very rapidly, but we really can hold only one thought in our mind at a time. Trying to think about more than one thing at once is very tiring and frustrating.

5. **Be selective.** The biggest weapon you have in fighting overwhelm is your ability to prioritize what you need to do. By making intelligent choices based upon categories such as urgent, non-urgent, important and non-important, we can focus better. Basing these choices on our core values, we can relax in the knowledge we're doing what matters most.

6. **Delegate.** Learn to gain the assistance of others. People like to help, but you have to ask. Anything that can be adequately done by someone else should be delegated. It's an important skill worth developing.

7. **Learn to say No.** Our feelings of overwhelm largely come from taking on too much. If you're asked to do something, don't be too quick to accept the assignment. You might think you're being a

nice person, but if you succumb to health problems because of it, you won't be nice for very much longer.

If you're *told* to do something (by a boss, for instance), ask them which things they would like to have you put off while you complete the new assignment.

8. **Take care of yourself.** There will always be times when we're called upon to put forth extra effort. And we can, if we've been taking good care of ourselves right along. For those periods where extra drive, a few extra hours and hard work are required, we need to be in good shape—mentally and physically.

    If we've been eating, sleeping and exercising properly, we'll be far better prepared for the extra stress our lives require.

    Remember to take breaks. The tendency for many of us is to work harder and longer. In actuality, we can get more done in less time and with less effort if we take breaks.

9. **Breathe.** When we feel overwhelmed, we have a tendency to tighten up instead of relax. It seems like there are many things we *have* to do, but the only thing we really have to do is breathe. Take some long deep breaths and feel yourself returning to the present.

10. **Focus on the task at hand.** If we're thinking about what's *not* getting done or all the other things we have to do, we can't focus well on what we're doing now. Think about what you *are* doing rather than what you're *not* getting done. Otherwise, you're going to be defeated by your feelings of overwhelm.

Use these ten tips in dealing with overwhelm, and you'll find yourself feeling more in charge and at peace.

"The secret of getting ahead is getting started. The secret of getting started is breaking your complex overwhelming tasks into small manageable tasks, and then starting on the first one."

—Mark Twain

42. Step Back and Gain New Perspective

I've owned several businesses in my career. And as I transitioned from one to another, I've always tried to review the experience to see what I could learn from it. I asked the question, "What Worked, What Didn't, and What's Next?"

As I performed these business reviews, I made notes about what I would have done differently. Sometimes I grew too fast, sometimes too slowly. I entered into contracts that weren't always prudent, spent too much money in some areas and not enough in others. I was often undercapitalized.

I also noted the things I thought we did well. And I learned from it all.

But the *one thing* I always wrote down that I would change was this: I would take more time off. Not just to play and relax—although I would have done that, too—but to gain a higher perspective.

What I would have done in every single business I've ever owned would be to step back away from the business—to work *on* the business as opposed to working solely *in* the business.

We all need to gain a better perspective than we can get from working down in the trenches. By getting out of our workday environment and asking elegant questions, we can see better where we are and where we're going.

Because of our economic times and the rapid rate of change, it's even more important to make sure our ladders are leaning against the right walls. And getting away is the best way to do this.

You can do it alone, but I find it works better if you can do it with someone else. Even two people can brainstorm problems, ask questions and look for unexploited opportunities.

A half- or full-day retreat with your staff can re-energize you and the entire team. It's a good change of pace; it lets them know what's going on; it gives you a chance to refocus everyone on the objectives and principles that matter most.

I like to ask: If I were starting today, how would I do it differently? What would I do that we're not doing now? What could we *stop* doing that's unnecessary?

All too often, we find ourselves doing tasks that have lost their value or meaning. By eliminating those things that aren't working very well or producing only minimal results, we free up time and energy to do the things that truly further our intentions.

This kind of thinking isn't always easy, but it's a lot easier than trying to do it while going about our day-to-day routine.

By taking a break and really looking objectively at our business, we can better understand what and why we're doing things. We can make better choices, become more profitable and enjoy the process more.

 Schedule your mini-retreat today. Start making notes about what you want to focus on—questions that will provide more insight, elegant choices and solutions. You won't regret it.

 SuccessNet's *Priorities*™ Tool is a great way to evaluate and prioritize your problems/opportunities—as well as your projects, goals and purchases.
www.SuccessNet.org/priorities.htm

"You must look within for value, but must look beyond for perspective."

—Denis Waitley

"In order to keep a true perspective of one's importance, everyone should have a dog that will worship them and a cat that will ignore them."

—unknown

"Never write about a place until you're away from it, because that gives you perspective."

—Ernest Hemingway

"Chicken Little acted before her research was complete."

— Charles Hendrickson Brower

43. Adventures in the Leaves

Each autumn, my wife Dawn and I do what many fall tourists in New England do. We take a leisurely drive around Vermont and watch the chlorophyll drain out of the leaves. The reds, yellows and oranges in early October are truly something to behold, and we enjoy ourselves immensely: talking, laughing and oohing and aahing our way around a good section of what we call the "Northeast Kingdom."

If you flattened out all the hills and mountains, Vermont would be a fairly good-sized state. But since it's hardly flat, it ranks down with the smallest of the fifty. Nonetheless, there are myriad back roads— roads that are easy to find, but not always so easy to find your way out of. Now I have a fairly keen sense of direction, and I almost always knew—at least roughly—where we were. Regardless, there were a number of times that our exact location was unknown until we emerged onto a road or scene that was more familiar. It was fun.

It occurred to me that in life, it's important we have a plan as to where we're going and equally important to have a sense of where we are. Although, if we know exactly where we're going, and precisely what's going to happen, there's no drama—no adventure.

In our trek around the highways and back roads of northern Vermont, we were willing to be a little lost because it added to the wonder of the experience. The *mission* was clear, but the plan was flexible. In other words, "set your goals in concrete and your plans in sand."

Too many people—myself included—have our lives so well scheduled and so tightly controlled, we forsake some of the spontaneous things that could add more spice, adventure and enjoyment. As I look back over my life, many of the things I labeled catastrophes turned out to be the proverbial blessing in disguise. Many of the things I initially looked upon as detours and delays added immeasurable quality to the journey.

I'm reminded of the story of the man who was discouraged and prayed that life would be easier and that he could win in every endeavor. One day, he was visited by an angel and his prayers were answered. Everything he touched turned to gold. No matter what he tried, it worked. Everything he wanted, he received—with no struggle and no fear of the end result. But, alas, he found himself miserable. Life was too predictable—like watching a taped football game to which you already know the outcome, it lacks excitement.

In a short while, the man prayed again—this time to be relieved of his wish. A second time he was visited by the angel, and the man said he would rather go to hell than continue with this "curse." The angel replied, "My son, hell is where you've been since we were last together."

We need to welcome the challenges and unknowns that come our way. They're what make us stronger and build our character. They are what provide the drama—the comedies and the tragedies—of our lives.

Be open and receptive to spontaneous developments in your life. Trust your intuition. Have the courage to do what isn't on the schedule.

Don't plan your life so tightly you can't take advantage of serendipitous events. Say yes to things outside of your comfort zone.

"Spontaneity is the quality of being able to do something just because you feel like it at the moment, of trusting your instincts, of taking yourself by surprise and snatching from the clutches of your well-organized routine, a bit of unscheduled plea."

—unknown

"The essence of pleasure is spontaneity."

—Germaine Greer

"Our whole life is an attempt to discover when our spontaneity is whimsical, sentimental irresponsibility and when it is a valid expression of our deepest desires and values."

—Helen Merell Lynd

44. Giving and Receiving

I know a young man who stands before the great "woodstove of life" and says, "Give me heat and I'll give you wood." For some reason, he feels the world owes him a livelihood with no regard for his contribution.

I'm not sure how he arrived at this point of view, but I know it's not working for him. He's outside the realm of proven universal principles and the results in his life reflect that.

And they always do. Wherever we're experiencing lack, we must look for what we've failed to give.

If you want more of something in your life, you need to give more of what you want.

Think about the people you respect and admire. Aren't they the ones who have given the most? Of course they are.

Cause and Effect

Some have referred to this principle as the Law of the Farm: In order to harvest in the fall, we must plant in the spring. We must give seed in order to have a crop.

But it's not a "tit-for-tat" equation.

The law is bigger than that. We get much *more* than we give. Why would we plant a kernel of corn to get back only another kernel? No, we plant a kernel to grow a stalk of corn that brings forth hundreds of kernels.

We all have something to give. We all have unique qualities and talents we can give to others.

We increase our value in the marketplace by bringing more value *to* the marketplace. It's really just that simple.

If we *want* more value in our life, then we must *give* more value. It might not show up as soon as we'd like and it might not return in the ways we thought it would. But rest assured, you cannot give without receiving. One is not even better than the other. They're just different parts of the same circle.

 Do you want more love in your life? Then give more love. Want more peace in your life? Then be more peaceful.

45. Give Yourself a Target

I played tennis with my 16-year-old son the other day. He's really coming along—hitting better and much more consistently.

He sure gets to the ball better than I do. But Kevin was having some trouble with his serve. He just wasn't getting it in with any real consistency.

I offered to help. I asked what his target was, and he replied it was the service box.

"That's too big," I said. "Your mind can't deal with 'getting it in.' It needs a more specific target."

I asked about his pitching (he's a talented baseball player) and asked where he aimed when he pitched. "Do you aim for the strike zone or a place *within* the strike zone?"

I could see he was thinking. I walked to the back edge of the service box and pointed to a spot about a foot inside. I said, "Aim for this." To this young man's credit, he not only accepted some coaching, but he was willing to try it.

And in spite of being tired and a bit frustrated, his service percentage went up *over 300 percent* from that point on. A target—a *specific* target—makes all the difference in the world.

Our minds—both subconscious and conscious—need to have something to shoot for. Vague generalities just won't work. We usually hit what we aim for—or at least we get a lot closer than we would have by *not* giving ourselves a clear target.

In the movie *The Patriot*, the hero played by Mel Gibson, reminds his young sons as they prepare to free their brother from the British, "Aim small, miss small." Good advice.

Make sure you know what you're aiming for. It can't be "success" unless you outline clearly what success is for you. It can't be excellent health unless you have a clear idea of what that looks like to you. It can't be wealth unless you can experience in your mind's eye what wealth will be.

 Have clear intentions. Get the picture. See it and experience it as vividly as you can. In doing so, you'll have an excellent chance to hit your mark.

46. I Love New York: A Positive Point of View

On a recent trip to NYC, I had breakfast with a colleague who said something that really made me stop and think.

Mike Foster (www.MikeFoster.com) holds the title of the top trainer out of 450 seminar leaders at a major international training organization. He's a dynamic, sought-after speaker and expert in what he calls e-Savvy—getting the most from your business technology.

In his profession, Mike travels three to four days a week, fifty weeks a year. He practically lives on a plane, and I asked this seasoned traveler what his favorite city was. The way he responded gave me pause.

Mike said he didn't have a favorite city. He didn't think it was a good idea to have favorites because that would take away from his enjoyment of the city he was in. "What if I never get back to that city for a couple of years?"

Mike was leaving later that morning for a training assignment in Chicago. He went on to say, "I love New York and I'm getting ready to love Chicago." Wow! What a positive way to look at things.

My astute breakfast companion was saying that even preferences can take us out of present time. Making judgments takes away from our enjoyment of where we are now.

It relates to one of the most profound things I've ever learned: It's our resistance to what *is* that creates our pain. Most, if not all, the emotional pain we experience in our lives is caused by our unwillingness to accept what is. Our belief that something isn't fair or somehow isn't right causes our upset and creates our pain. Being able to accept the things we cannot change is the only path to peace. And someone with pure acceptance is a rare individual indeed.

Longing to have something other than what we have reduces the value of our current experience. Our energy and resourcefulness is depleted when we pine for where we want to go.

Mike's philosophy was particularly important to me because, for a variety of reasons, our trip to New York was less than ideal. In fact, it was the worst trip my wife and I have ever taken. It seemed that almost everything that could go wrong did. It took every bit of our positive attitudes to make the best of it.

I wasn't at a point where I could quite say, "I love New York," but Mike certainly helped me think about things with a higher perspective than I would have otherwise. I did my best to milk the value from a trip that most would have labeled a disaster.

By not labeling, by not judging—even in *little* ways—you can enhance your life dramatically. The fact is, you can't afford to complain about things. When you judge things as bad or wrong and especially when you complain about them, you keep your focus on what you don't want. And what you focus on expands.

"The reason people find it so hard to be happy is that they always see the past better than it was, the present worse than it is, and the future less resolved than it will be."

—Marcel Pagnol

"True happiness is . . . to enjoy the present, without anxious dependence upon the future."

—Seneca

"I love my past, I love my present. I am not ashamed of what I have had, and I am not sad because I no longer have it."

—Sidonie Gabrielle Colette

"People who live in the past generally are afraid to compete in the present. I've got my faults, but living in the past is not one of them. There's no future in it."

—Sparky Anderson

47. Staying on Track

One of the most important things SuccessNet does is to help people stay on track in being their best. Pretty much everything we do is targeted toward that goal.

Anyone can do the things necessary to be successful and accomplish their goals. The challenge is to do them consistently.

And that's what separates the winners from the also-rans. Staying on track day in and day out is what it takes to weave successful days into a successful life.

So how do we stay on track? How do we remain motivated and focused toward our highest and best?

Allow me to share with you a few things that have worked for me. Perhaps they can help you stay on track.

Three Most Important Goals
I have many goals. I always have a few dozen I'm working toward. But I keep three first and foremost in my mind. Every day I know I must do something that will help me make progress toward their achievement.

I look at these goals every day. They're never out of my consciousness. And I usually take action every day on each of these three goals.

What's Next?
Martin Sheen's character in the hit TV series *The West Wing* is President Jeb Bartlett. His way of saying he's done with something and ready to move on is to ask the question, "What's next?"

It's a good question to ask ourselves. Not only what's next, but what's the most important thing we can do today to move us closer to our most important objectives.

Keep Your Goals in Front of You
Put pictures of your goals up so you see them often. Review them regularly, but most importantly, review the *reasons* why you want to accomplish these goals. It's the reasons that will make the difference.

Talk About Your Goals with Supportive People
Having a Master Mind group is ideal. If you don't have one, you can still share your goals with people who will encourage and support you. And you can do the same for them.

By talking about your goals, you make them more real. You'll also get ideas from others on how you can better achieve them. People can't help you if they don't know what you want.

Forgive Yourself and Move On

Way too much emotional energy and thinking is wasted because we keep reviewing past behaviors. The past is gone. Today is all we have. Don't squander time and energy thinking about what you should have done, could have done, what you did or might have done.

Today is a new day. Move on. The point of power is in the present.

Affirmation and Visualization

Affirmative statements and visualizing the achievement of our goals help us to "feel" our way to success. Anything we can do to elevate our emotional connection with our objectives will help us stay on track.

It's well worth developing strategies that work to keep us consistently moving toward our goals. As we do so, we build a track record of success. And setting and achieving bigger goals becomes even easier.

48. Your Agreements Show Your Integrity

Except for disease and climatic disasters, I believe over 90 percent of the world's problems result from people not keeping their agreements.

Think about it. From countries to corporations to families and friends, most every upset—little or large—can be traced back to someone not keeping their end of the bargain.

Wars break out, companies fail, marriages end, friendships fracture and deals fall through simply because of broken agreements.

We all make agreements every day. Some seem small and insignificant: an agreed-upon time to meet, a promise to run an errand. Others are seen as bigger and more important: a formal contract or signing a loan agreement.

All of them are important because this is the way trust is earned. A person's reputation is built upon their ability to make and keep agreements.

Your life—and the lives of those around you—will work better when agreements are carefully made and diligently kept. The quality of your life is in direct relation to the quality of your agreements.

Here are seven tips to help you become and remain a person who can be counted upon:

1. **Take All Agreements Seriously**
    When you agree to do something—do it. And do it when you said you would in the way you agreed to do it. When you agree to meet someone, be sure to be there and be on time. Agreements with yourself matter, too. If you promise yourself that you'll exercise today, keep your promise. Develop the *habit* of keeping your agreements.

2. **Be Careful What You Agree To**
    Don't give your word lightly. Many people find it easier to say Yes instead of No. But it's far better to be a bit guarded with what we agree to do, because we can find ourselves getting over-committed and then unable to complete what we said we would.

3. **Keep Track of Your Agreements**
    In the course of a week, we might enter into dozens of agreements. We must have some way to track these promises—a follow-up system to keep yourself—and those you deal with—on top of what was promised. Write them down. You may have great

intentions, but if you forget to do what you agreed to do, the result is the same as you *choosing* not to keep your agreement.

4. **Make Sure Your Agreements are Clear**
   With a written agreement you have a prayer. With a verbal agreement you've got nothing but air. It's always best to have a written agreement—even if it's just a letter or a note of understanding. It's much easier to iron out any confusion later if it was written down, and no one has to rely on the memory of a conversation.

5. **Be Careful With Whom You Make Agreements**
   There's an old adage, "Cheat me once, shame on you; cheat me twice, shame on me." If you make agreements with people who have a history of not keeping them, you're leaving yourself wide open for disappointment.

6. **Renegotiate When You're Unable to Keep Your Agreement**
   When you find yourself unable or unwilling to complete an agreement, always go to the other party or parties and renegotiate. It may be uncomfortable, but it will keep you in integrity and has far more class than simply not addressing the issue.

7. **Manage by Agreement**
   Instead of just telling someone to do something, ask them if they would agree to doing X by such and such time. If I tell someone to do something, they might do it because they were told to do so. But if I ask them and gain their agreement, I've got a lot better chance that it'll get done. In using this method, you also find out if your request was clearly understood.

By paying careful attention to the agreements we make, by tracking them and developing the habit of keeping all our agreements, we become and remain a person of integrity.

Our lives and the world around us work in direct proportion to the quality of our agreements.

49. Metrics Make a Difference

*You Can't Change What You
Don't Measure and Understand*

Every enterprise has important numbers that should be monitored—and they're not all financial.

If you operate a business, you're required to maintain certain financial records in order to properly report your income and pay taxes. But most of these financials are too historic to really make good management decisions.

What's needed are good metrics related to the most important things that affect our desired outcomes. By tracking the right metrics, we can affect the changes we need to make in order to be successful.

Interestingly enough, the simple act of measuring things seems to alter the numbers in the right direction. What we focus on expands, and if we focus on the right things, we'll start to see those numbers change the way we'd like them to change.

Every business is different, and it's up to us to determine what needs measuring and how best to do it. Try brainstorming about what activities could be measured and then select those you think would be the most meaningful. If they prove not to be so valuable, try some others.

In a small business, paying people based on metrics rather than profits is usually much more effective. If you buy a new Mercedes, and it's a business expense, your incentives based on profit sharing are adversely affected. But if you base bonuses on agreed-upon metrics, the payoff and increased performance for employees occurs sooner. And it's usually more fair.

Even if you're not a business owner, you can find the best metrics to monitor what you do in your job. In doing so, you'll be able to track things better and make changes that impact those numbers in a positive fashion. You can increase your own productivity, as well as that of your business, and everyone becomes more valuable.

Metrics work. Metrics matter. Metrics will make a difference if you use them. Because you *can* change what you measure and understand.

Here's an acrostic to help remember what good metrics can do for us:

Measure
Essentials
To
Rapidly
Increase
Clarity and
Success

Clarity leads to power and the right metrics will gain that clarity for us.

Keep your metrics simple and easy to record and you'll do more of it. Make a game out of it. The easier it is to do and the more fun it is, the more likely you are to follow through with this powerful process.

Programs like Excel and Access enable you to easily chart and graph your numbers so they become more meaningful and allow you to spot important trends.

You can even develop important metrics for your personal goals. Create ways to track the action steps needed to achieve your goals, and you'll achieve them more easily and consistently. Monitor your income, outgo, net worth, exercise program, diet, weight—anything that moves you toward your objectives.

50. Get What You Want!

I've learned as much from my kids as I've taught them—probably more. I learned this particular lesson from my oldest son Mike.

The year was 1994. Mike was in the Marine Corps and home on a short leave. I was in the throws of buying my first "real" computer. I'd been using personal computers for over ten years, but I'd never gone online. We hadn't bought a new computer since Windows debuted, and we were still using DOS.

Not being entirely sure how I was going to put this new computer to good use, I was having a hard time justifying the purchase. It felt like a big decision. And at the time, it seemed like a big expense for our family. Nevertheless, I still had a feeling that it was the right thing to do.

We were shopping at an electronics store, and I was showing Mike some of the different machines I was considering. I explained the different features and tradeoffs that were part of my decision.

I shared that I was about to buy one that was close to what I wanted. It didn't have all the features of the one I truly desired, but it was cheaper, and I was going to save a couple hundred dollars.

Mike looked at me in kind of a quizzical way and said, "Dad, get what you *want!*"

His perspective was refreshing. I was agonizing over a fairly paltry amount of money—especially over the two to four years I expected to own the computer. My son, in his wisdom, helped me give myself the permission to not settle for something less.

When we settle, we're telling ourselves we're not worth it. We're affirming a belief in lack instead of abundance. We're saying we don't believe in ourselves enough to have what we really want.

I bought the more expensive computer and was happy I did. Given that I view my life from *before* being online and *after* being online, it was a profitable decision, too.

I firmly believe the Universe takes care of us about as well as we take care of ourselves. There's something about feeling worthy that opens doors we never would have even seen before.

I know for a fact that as a result of taking better care of myself, I've had a lot more to give—and have given more—than I used to.

Certainly we can take this "self-indulgence" to extremes, and I'm definitely not advocating giving in to our every whim and fancy. Even now, I tend to be a fairly conservative shopper, and I rarely buy frivolous things. When I trade up, I still buy computers about six months behind the technology curve, and we save a fair amount in doing so.

But I do treat myself a lot better than I did before. I don't need a lot of "things" in my life. And the things I do have, I want to be able to appreciate and enjoy. I want to love having them.

That event and my son's statement have stayed with me over the years. I often recall it when I'm not being particularly kind or generous to myself. It's a valuable lesson.

"When you recover or discover something that nourishes your soul and brings joy, care enough about yourself to make room for it in your life."
—Jean Shinoda Bolen

"The name of the game is taking care of yourself, because you're going to live long enough to wish you had."
—Grace Mirabella

"The world is full of abundance and opportunity, but far too many people come to the fountain of life with a sieve instead of a tank car . . . a teaspoon instead of a steam shovel. They expect little and as a result they get little."
—Ben Sweetland

51. When is it Great Enough?

For the past few weeks, my wife and I have been putting the finishing touches on my latest book. We've been proofing, revising, editing and even swapping out chapters. Finally, we proclaimed it "complete." It's often a tough call—particularly when it's your "baby."

Most projects can be fiddled with, tweaked, polished and revised to the point where they never actually get done. For many people, this can be a way to keep from failing. If the book, thesis or work of art is always in progress, then no one will judge it. What looks like a desire for perfection is often simply fear of failure.

I expect there are many of you reading this who are close to finishing something dear to you, but you seem to find excuses for not bringing the project to completion. Perhaps you have a number of unfinished projects.

Remember that nothing is ever perfect. You'll always think of ways you could have made it better, sleeker, more efficient and with additional features.

But I like what my friend Mike Litman says, "You don't have to get it perfect, you just have to get it going."

Get it launched. Get it working. You can improve upon it later. Anything worthwhile is worth improving upon. All great things are in a constant state of improvement.

With the exception of a few things like brain surgery, airline maintenance and nuclear power plants, it's safe to say that something complete, but imperfect, has infinitely more value than something almost perfect but never done.

As for my new book, we could still be working on it. But that wouldn't put it in your hands or in the hands of thousands of others next month. It can't accomplish its purpose if it never gets printed. Will we find corrections and improvements we'll want to make? For sure. That's what second editions are for.

At some point you have to say, "It's great enough."

 What ideas, projects or creations are you procrastinating about? Could it be you're afraid it won't be perfect?

Almost everything can be improved upon after its debut. So don't let your desire to get it perfect keep you from getting it going.

If you haven't started, start. If you haven't finished, finish.

52. What Does He/She Really Want?

Clarity does lead to power. And knowing what you really want is critical to achieving your highest and best.

But do you truly know what your spouse wants from you? Do you really know what your employee or your boss wants from you? And are you clear about what you want from *them*?

My wife and I just spent another memorable weekend on Lake Champlain. The weather was great, the food was delicious, and of course, the company was excellent.

One of the things that made it even more special was a deep and intense conversation that resulted from two simple questions about which we decided to dialog.

Dawn and I have a great relationship, and after 11 years together, we feel we know each other very well. And we also believe we can make our relationship better and understand each other better.

Before we left on our overnight trip, we decided to individually list the answers to two questions.

1. What do I want, or want more of, from Michael/Dawn?
2. What I *don't* want, or want less of, from Michael/Dawn?

Then after dinner, in the cozy cockpit of "Attitude," with a beautiful sunset as a backdrop, we began our dialog.

Our plan was to each offer one of our answers from both questions. We then discussed them in detail. It made all the difference in the world to have this discussion when we were both open and receptive, rather than when we were tired, upset or stressed—which, in most relationships, is when these discussions take place.

We had several ahas, some new insights, *much* greater clarity and the chance to be more loving to one another.

I highly recommend this simple process for anyone wanting to create a better relationship. It provides the opportunity to love and care for the other person in the way they would like to be loved and cared for.

 Try it and see for yourself. I'm sure you'll discover things you didn't expect and realize assumptions you've made that were erroneous. The end result is greater understanding, more intimacy and more fun.

53. Handling Frustrations

"I'm sooo frustrated!" These words—or something perhaps even more colorful—are things we've all said at one time or another. Several times over the past few days, I said them myself—at least in my head.

We recently incorporated a new computer into our network, and it raised all kinds of havoc. An installation that should have taken only a few hours turned into a three-day exercise in aggravation and frustration.

In our recent experience, my wife and I dealt with it better than we thought we would have. We never lost our patience with one another, and we were never rude to each other or the people we worked with in resolving the problems.

As I look at what happened, I can see things that allowed us to get through the installation with no upset. Here are what I see as the key strategies we used—although not perfectly—to avoid being victims of the experience.

Emotional Bank Accounts

One of the things that made our recent ordeal more bearable was that my wife and I had high balances in our respective "emotional bank accounts." When these bank balances are low, the little things can easily become big things. Little "forgotten" resentments can turn into major issues. By making daily deposits into our emotional bank accounts with people we're close to, we can avoid having unnecessary upsets make a difficult situation hurtful.

Ask Good Questions

When we get frustrated, it's easy to ask fruitless, impotent questions—questions that exacerbate the situation rather than improve upon it.

Questions like, "Why did this happen to me?" "Why is life so unfair?" "Why are people so unreasonable?" are the kind of questions that keep us stuck and feeling unresourceful. We need to ask questions that move us forward. Keep asking, "What's really important?"

Stay Focused—Identify the Problem

In the midst of a crisis (whether perceived or real), it's easy to lose our focus. We have to keep coming back to what the problems are and what we can do to solve them.

As the experience and drama unfolds, stay with the intended result and keep redefining the problem.

Take a Break

It's important to take breaks. Don't become obsessed with the problem(s) and keep at it without any let-up. We can't be at our best when we operate non-stop without a chance to step back and gain some perspective—and rest.

Stop. Get some exercise. Take a walk. Work out. Take a nap. Watch a movie. You'll be surprised how much more resourceful you can be. In the whole scheme of things, how much difference will a few minutes (or hours) make?

Remember to breathe. As someone once said, "Inspiration is the art of breathing in."

Perspective

Keep in mind that frustration is an emotional reaction. It doesn't happen "out there," it happens inside us. And we have choice about whether we indulge it.

Be aware. Notice when you're feeling frustrated. Don't judge it. Blaming ourselves or others will not work. Ninety percent of overcoming the problem is your conscious awareness that you're stressed. Ask yourself, "In three years' time, will this situation be worth being upset?" Chances are, it won't.

Laugh

We stress ourselves out by taking things too seriously. Being serious doesn't mean we have to be grim. Learn to laugh at yourself as well as the situation. The things that seem upsetting now will usually be things we'll find humorous later. If we're going to laugh about it then, we might as well laugh about it now.

Get Help

Going through any challenging situation is more bearable and often more fun when we experience it with a friend or team member. Ask for help. Where is it written that you need to go it alone?

What was the end result of that week's computer fiasco? Well, one of our publications was delayed two days, and it's doubtful anyone noticed. We learned a lot. And, we ended up with a better system than we'd originally planned because we exchanged the first computer for a better one.

54. Set Smart Goals

Goal setting is a skill. And, unfortunately, it's not something that's usually taught in school. Studies have shown that less than three percent of people actually write their goals down. And it's this *same* three percent who accomplish more than all the others put together.

If you want to get better at setting and achieving goals, here's an acronym that will help you focus and have more success reaching your objectives.

Set **SMART** goals. SMART stands for:

> **S**pecific
>
> **M**easurable
>
> **A**ction-oriented
>
> **R**ealistic
>
> **T**imely

Specific
Achieving goals demands focus. Our minds need specific targets to work effectively. They can't operate well with vague generalities. State exactly what you wish to accomplish.

Measurable
Many people set goals they'll never know whether or not they've attained. "To be successful—to be more knowledgeable," aren't goals because there's no benchmark. Be sure to have *measurable* goals.

Action-oriented
It's much easier to measure things being done. What are the action steps you'll take in the process of achieving your goal?

Realistic
This is your call. What's realistic to you may not be to someone else. Your objective has to be within the realm of *your* believability. If you can't envision yourself doing it, you won't.

Timely
A goal must have a target date. If you desire to make a million dollars, but don't set the timeline for it, it won't be motivating. A deadline too far in the future is too easily put off. A goal that's set too close is not only unrealistic, it's discouraging.

If you keep these things in mind as you plan your goals, you'll meet with more success and have more fun doing so.

55. Listen, Pause, Clarify and Validate

Our ability to communicate effectively is one of the most precious skills we can develop. Most of the time, when we think of communicating well, we think of effectively expressing ourselves. This is certainly important, but listening is the single most important of all communication skills. It's what Stephen Covey calls "Seek first to understand and then to be understood."

Listen

First and foremost, we must actively listen to what someone is saying. Perhaps we were given two ears and one mouth because we were supposed to listen twice as much as we speak. Look at the person who is speaking. Listen with your whole body and your whole mind. Resist the temptation to think about your response. People will appreciate your respectful listening.

Pause

This is a great habit to develop. When the speaker is finished, pause for a few seconds before responding. This guarantees that the other person has really finished talking, and there is no danger of cutting them off. By pausing, we show the speaker that we've listened to them, and we respect what they had to say enough to consider it before we launch into our response.

Clarify

You could call this "Backtrack and Clarify." This is where you rephrase what was said and ask if you understood correctly. You get agreement as to the communication, and you make sure that what you heard was really what was meant. It takes only a moment and prevents assumptions that create misunderstandings later.

Validate

This is the one I've had the most trouble with. After we have clarified, we validate the opinion/feeling/expression of the other.

Validation does not necessarily mean agreement. It simply means we understand how they might feel or think about something. And if you *were* them, and had the same experience, you *would* feel or think like them.

This whole process might seem like it would be time consuming, but it's really not. Even if it takes a little longer at first, you'll find it makes for clearer, more effective communication with less hurt feelings and more understanding. Something the world needs a lot more of.

56. Is Your Relationship a Ten?

Building and maintaining a great relationship with someone is an all-the-time endeavor.

The following simple process is one you can use for *any* relationship—personal, professional, coworker, boss, friend or business partner.

If we really care about a relationship, we have to regularly check on how we're doing. We can't depend upon the other party to always tell us what's working and what's not.

Here's the sequence: Ask them, "On a scale of one to ten, how would you rate our relationship?" And then wait for the answer. If they're slow to respond, you may want to jump into the silence. Resist that temptation.

If they rate your relationship anything less than ten, ask, "What would it take to make it a ten?" Again, it's worth the wait for answers that will give you important insight into what the other person wants and needs.

Assumptions can wound or even kill the best of relationships. These simple questions can keep assumptions from hurting your relationship and help you develop a deeper, more fulfilling one.

It may seem uncomfortable at first, but it gets easier. It's often a conversation that will continue over several sessions. It's a great springboard for some in-depth discussions, so get ready for some breakthroughs.

Go ahead and ask the question: "On a scale of one to ten, how would you rate our relationship?" Listen carefully.

If they rate your relationship anything less than ten, ask, "What would it take to make it a ten?"

As we like to say, "feedback is the breakfast of champions," and using this process can only help you win.

"Personal relationships are the fertile soil from which all advancement, all success, all achievement in real life grows."

—Ben Stein

57. There's No Limit to Prosperity

Cable News Headline: "Oil Prices Rise, but the Economy is Unstoppable"

I'm not an economist, but it sure seems to me that the above headline is right on. The economy *is* unstoppable. It's huge and getting bigger. I still maintain we're at the beginning of the largest economic boom in the history of the world.

One of the limiting beliefs held by many—either consciously or unconsciously—is that there is a finite supply of money. In other words, if one person has more, then that means someone else has less. It's simply not true, and the following story illustrates the point well.

Back in the eighties, Steven Rockefeller built a house in Cornwall, Vermont. It was reported to have cost a million dollars. Back then, a million-dollar home in Vermont was quite rare. It was a beauty.

My friend John Cady was one of the best commercial painters in northern Vermont, and he was fortunate enough to be awarded the painting contract for the Rockefeller mansion. I always thought it was interesting he was paid by checks written on account number ONE of the Chase Manhattan Bank.

Stay with me, here, as we see how wealth was not only moved to Vermont but also how it created even *more* wealth.

Before the house was built, Rockefeller had a million dollars in his family's bank in New York. After the house was built, he still had his million dollars; it's just that now it's in the form of a house. He exchanged his interest-earning million dollars for a million-dollar appreciating asset—his home.

Now here's where it gets interesting. This was not an even exchange. The million dollars was transformed—cash into real estate. But there was *also* now a million dollars in cash in the hands of contractors and building suppliers. That million was circulating through the Vermont economy and beyond.

A million dollars became two million dollars in the course of only a few months. Wealth was not only transferred—it was *created*.

That's the power of the economy. And there's no limit to the wealth and prosperity that can be created.

58. Financial Independence

Financial independence, by its very definition, means to not be dependent on anyone or anything for our financial needs. That requires being free from debt.

When asked what they would do if they won the lottery, most people say they would pay off their debts.

We'd all like to be free from owing money. But something has happened to us over the past couple of generations—we've come to accept debt as just another part of modern life.

It doesn't have to be that way.

The average American will earn between $600,000 and $2,000,000 in his or her lifetime. But it's not important what we make—it's what we keep that makes the difference. The percentage of people reaching 65, who are financially independent, are in the small single digits. Over 25 percent of the U.S. federal budget is used just to pay interest on the national debt. Debt has become the new "American Way," and it's not something to be proud of.

Bankruptcies, failed marriages, alcohol and drug abuse, crime and a host of other problems can often be related to the scourge of debt. Part of the reason we've embraced being in debt for most, if not all, of our lives can be attributed to the fact that everyone else— including our government—is doing it. Owing one, two or even three times as much as we earn in a year would have been horrifying to our grandparents. Had consumer debt—a term unheard of only 30 years ago—not crept into our society gradually, it never would have been embraced.

Just think what it would be like if you owed absolutely nothing to anyone for anything. All the payments you pay each month—all the interest, all the worry, the limited choices—would disappear. No more would you have to stay in a job or a profession you despise with people you don't respect. You would feel not only free from debt but would experience freedom in many other aspects of your life.

Imagine what your life would be like if you only had to pay for utilities, food and entertainment. Would it make a difference in the quality of your life, the quality of your relationships, your health? Of course it would.

We can all become debt-free and in less time than you might think. But first we have to get serious about it. It won't happen by itself. The 40-40-40 plan won't cut it. That's working 40 hours a week,

40 years of your life and retiring at 40 percent of what you were making before.

Most people work into May of each year just to pay their taxes to the state and federal government. How many more months do we have to work to pay the interest and principle payments on what we owe?

Let's say you owe $40,000—not counting your home mortgage—credit cards, furniture, cars, etc. If the average interest on this debt was 14 percent, you'd have to pay $5,600 just in interest each year. On top of that, of course, are principle payments. That could easily be another $5,000 to $10,000. Even if you were only paying $10,000 in payments on this debt, you would have to make over $13,000 before taxes to service this liability. If you made $35,000 annually, you'd be working almost five months of the year just to make your payments. Add to that the five months to pay taxes and what have you got left? Is that any way to live? No wonder so many people feel trapped.

How Do You Get There?

Getting out of debt and staying out of debt is simple. *Simple*, but not easy. I want to encourage and support you and your businesses to become debt-free. I'm confident you'll have more fun, encounter less stress and be more productive.

My wife and I have made our plan, we've simplified our lives, and we are well on our way to reaching this objective. Our company has no debt, and we'll personally be free of all debt in a short while. You can do it, too.

Debt-Free, then Wealth

Albert Einstein was once asked what he considered to be the greatest invention of all time. "Compound interest," was his reply.

When you've eliminated your debts, you can then start to use this "great invention" and make compound interest work *for* you instead of *against* you. You will develop an investment portfolio that can make you truly wealthy in only a few years. You can become a true capitalist in the real sense of the word—one who creates capital. And you will be free.

You owe it to yourself and those you love to free yourself from the power-robbing, creativity-stifling, worry-causing scourge of debt. After that, you can begin to develop real wealth.

59. Keep Moving

The sailboat was coming slowly into the marina under power. There was a south wind blowing about 15-20 knots, and it was beginning to rain. The helmsman appeared confident and had several crew aboard, so I elected not to walk over to the other dock and offer assistance. But I kept an eye out just in case.

As the skipper made the turn into his slip he slowed even more—so much so that he stopped. It was then that the wind pushed his bow around and, before his crew could fend off, slammed it into the end of the dock. With another go-around, they recovered and eventually tied up safe and secure. The hull's gel coat probably wasn't damaged nearly as much as the pride of her skipper.

Always wanting to learn from my own or others' mistakes, I thought about what happened and how it could have been avoided. In my opinion, this skipper violated one of the basic principles of seamanship: keep the boat moving.

In his well-intended effort to be cautious, he lost steerage because the boat stopped its forward motion. Without water flowing past the rudder, he had no ability to direct his vessel. You don't need much headway, but you need enough to make the rudder responsive—to maintain control.

Our lives are not ships, but it's a good metaphor. Safe in harbor, we need times of rest and reflection where action is not required. But in the marketplace, when we take action, we need to be doing enough to give us headway—enough to guide and control our forward motion—to maintain momentum.

When we're moving ahead, we see things we wouldn't see at rest. We experience events that otherwise wouldn't have occurred. Oftentimes, the goal we start out to accomplish turns out not to be what we wanted but instead leads us along our true path. All because of our forward motion.

A universal principle states that, "a body in motion tends to remain in motion." Conversely, a body at rest tends to remain at rest. And as we saw in the story of the sailboat, we can be blown about by all manner of things that can, and most often are, contrary to our intention.

When we rest, we should rest, but when the time comes for action, *keep moving*!

60. What's in Your Toolbox?

Think tools are just for carpenters and plumbers? Think again!

Everyone has a toolbox—or *should* have.

We each pick up tools that will help us survive as we move through our lives. We fill our own personal toolboxes with the tools that help us acquire what we need, build what we want, overcome our obstacles and find our way.

Lawyers have certain tools that help them research, analyze and express an argument clearly. Moms use tools that help them stay on track, focused and balanced. CEO's use specific tools—as do entrepreneurs.

Whether you're aware of it or not, *you* have a toolbox, too. Are your tools useful and up-to-date? Do they help you to just survive, or do they help you to thrive?

One of the hallmarks of a successful person is a toolbox full of relevant, practical and handy tools. Successful people consciously fill their toolbox with tools that fit the specific job.

We all know what it's like to attempt a job without the right tools. It's frustrating at best and downright futile at worst.

Tools enable us to leverage our talents and abilities so we can do more than we could otherwise.

The tools we're referring to are anything that helps us accomplish our intended outcomes. And the tools we can immediately think of that help us do this are:

computer	phone	programs
library	checklists	calculator
mastermind	team	email
teleconferences	personal network	

 Fill your personal toolbox for success. What are the tools of *your* trade? What do you need to do your job—to succeed in your life and career? What systems allow you to leverage yourself? What equipment do you need? What references, information or relationships will you need to achieve your goals?

 For a list of tools to help you operate at your personal and professional best, go to www.SuccessNet.org/tools.htm

61. Faster than the Speed of Thought

One of the ways you can differentiate yourself in the marketplace is to deliver your products and services faster than your competition.

I just signed off on the proofs for a 300-page book with a full-color cover. The turnaround for this digital printer is less than eight days—and most of that is spent sending and receiving proofs. Compare that to a four- to six-week process for most offset book printers. There are even printers who now produce books one at a time—as they're needed. It's called Print on Demand.

More and more customers want quick—or even immediate—delivery.

Fred Smith launched an entire industry with his idea for FedEx and overnight delivery. Now it's commonplace. Domino's Pizza may not be the *best* pizza, but it's known for delivering good, hot pizza within 30 minutes.

The old adage, "Good things take time," isn't entirely true anymore. And when we find ways to provide services faster, we're able to stand above the crowd.

No matter what you do, there's almost always a way to deliver your product faster and save time and money—while increasing customer attraction and loyalty.

Hardly a day goes by without someone telling us how much they appreciate how quickly we respond to their requests. They're surprised when we reply within a few hours—oftentimes minutes.

I can only assume they're surprised because they're not used to this kind of service. And yet, it should be the norm rather than the exception.

Just because it's always been done a certain way doesn't mean it can't be done differently. Perhaps there's an approval process that can be streamlined—or even eliminated. Maybe you can have processes happen simultaneously instead of consecutively.

Where does the "wait" happen? What can be done ahead of time? How can you anticipate the choices your customer will likely make?

These are all questions that will lead to breakthroughs and cause innovation to occur. If you're looking to be known for speed—if you're looking for ways to save time and money—it will happen. You can be known for quality *and* speed.

62. The Art of Gratefulness

"If you learn to appreciate more of what you already have, you'll find yourself having more to appreciate."

The word appreciate has several meanings. One is to be thankful or show gratitude. Another is to raise or increase in value—such as how a good investment appreciates with time. I think that by appreciating—practicing gratefulness—the things we have and want in our lives also increase.

In our hectic, fast-paced lives, it's easy to forget about the many things for which we have to be grateful. We tend to be goal-seeking, achievement-oriented people.

And there's nothing wrong with that.

However, it's vitally important that we not lose sight of the things that are near and dear—things we all too easily take for granted.

What we focus on expands. If we focus on the problems in our lives, they tend to increase. If we focus on the good things we already have, they too, have a tendency to grow.

I see it as another form of prayer. When we worry and fret over things, we make them bigger than they really are, as well as attract more of the same. That's negative prayer—prayer in reverse.

Focusing on what we *have* and what we *want* "appreciates" these things—they grow.

 Just before going to sleep each night, my wife and I share at least three things for which we're thankful. We call it "doing our gratefuls." It takes only a few moments, but it directs our thoughts on the good—on the things we wish to increase in our life.

I suggest making the conscious consideration of your blessings a daily occurrence. If you do, you'll find them taking on an even greater presence.

"Each day offers us the gift of being a special occasion, if we can simply learn that as well as giving, it is blessed to receive with grace and a grateful heart."

—Sarah Ban Breathnach

63. Never Give Up!

After World War II ended, Winston Churchill was invited to give the commencement address at Oxford University. You can imagine the anticipation and excitement felt by that graduating class when they found out the most famous person living at that time was to be their speaker.

When the great orator was introduced, he walked slowly to the platform, took off his top hat and set it down. He leaned his cane against the podium and looked silently into the faces of each of the graduates.

After a long while, he said in his crisp and commanding British accent, "Never give up." He then waited quietly, letting the full impact of his words sink into the consciousness of his listeners while they waited intently for what he was to say next.

A full minute—a very long time for a speaker to say nothing—reigned before he uttered his next sentence. His voice boomed even more loudly this time, punctuating each word, "Never give up!"

His words resonated powerfully through those hallowed halls and the minds of those present. Another ninety seconds went by before he spoke again. "Never give up!"

With that, he picked up his cane and his top hat and walked from the stage.

It's probably the only commencement address ever given that every student in attendance could remember word for word. It must have had even greater impact for those who had endured the bombing of London and the five years of war with Germany.

For it was Winston Churchill who said at the beginning of the war, "We will fight on the beaches, we shall fight on the landing grounds, we shall fight in the fields and in the streets. We shall fight in the hills; we shall never surrender."

Giving up was never an option for Churchill and it was that steadfast commitment which provided the ability to persevere and eventually triumph over Hitler's evil war machine.

We can all heed Churchill's famous advice. I'm not saying that there aren't times that giving up on something isn't the right move.

But there are some things that should never be surrendered. There are things near and dear to us that should never be compromised. Freedom is certainly one of them.

We're fortunate to live with great political freedom. But what about financial freedom? Many of us feel in bondage of some sort. Perhaps it's in bondage to a drug, a job, a relationship. It doesn't matter what it is. If it prevents us from being all that we are, we are—to some degree—slaves to someone or something else.
Our fathers and forefathers fought for our political freedom. We owe it to them and to our children to fight for our freedom to live without burdening debt, to do the work of our choosing, to live where we want to live and be as we wish to be—to be fully free!

On that, we must never give up.

———————

"Men do not fail . . . they give up trying."

—unknown

"Things don't go wrong and break your heart so you can become bitter and give up. They happen to break you down and build you up so you can be all that you were intended to be."

—Charlie "Tremendous" Jones

64. Are You Efficient *and* Effective?

People often ask me how I get so much done. Most are surprised to learn SuccessNet has no full-time employees except me, and they wonder how we can serve nearly 100,000 subscribers and produce so much material. Sometimes I wonder, too.

I feel that overall, I'm pretty efficient. I've learned many ways to multi-task and have developed skills, tools and habits that make life easier. But I've still got a lot to learn, and I'm constantly looking for ways to get more done in less time with greater enjoyment. I want to be more *effective*.

You see, efficiency just isn't enough. According to the dictionary, being efficient means acting or producing something with a minimum of waste, expense or unnecessary effort—exhibiting a high ratio of output to input.

But effectiveness is, in my opinion, about creating an intended outcome—one that has meaning and purpose. It's about getting the important things done—the ones with the biggest payoff.

And that's where we often fall down. We might be efficient in doing tasks that are simply not the most important work to be done. We must use our power of focus and discernment to be doing what will matter most.

It's easy to fool ourselves into thinking we're being productive, when in actuality, we're just being busy. We might get some immediate satisfaction, but in the long run, we'll not be achieving our goals as effectively as we could.

Having a powerful purpose, strong core values, clear goals and then establishing priorities for our tasks will make the difference. All the highly effective people I've encountered have mastered most, if not all, of these factors.

They make consistent progress and get more done than others who don't employ these principles. It's actually pretty simple—not always easy—but simple, nonetheless.

All it takes is some thinking, some clarity and some willingness to disentangle ourselves from habits and routines that no longer serve us.

Are you willing to make that investment of time?

65. We Named Her "Attitude"

The boat we have now is the third boat I've owned. But it's the first one I've ever given a name.

It was an interesting process. The list was long and there were many good ones, but we soon realized that both my wife and I had veto power, coming up with one we agreed upon wasn't going to be easy.

We wanted a name that really meant something to us and about our work—something distinctive. Some of the names we thought of were a bit too cute—like "Member Ship" and "A Mission." (I figured if I was sailing, someone could say I was on "A Mission.") Some others were just too common—like "Odyssey" or "Carpe Diem."

In the end, we decided that "Attitude" was the one we liked the most.

Of all the principles and ideologies we teach—some profound, some just plain practical—attitude is a big one.

I give a great deal of credit to my successes to having a good attitude. When I lost everything in a business failure over 20 years ago, I told people I left with only two things—my rhododendron plant and my attitude. I don't know where the plant went, but I've maintained my attitude pretty well over the years—even through some very dark times.

I don't have much patience for people with poor attitudes. I recognize everybody has bad days, but you can tell a lot about somebody by how they act when things aren't going well.

Being around people with good attitudes is a joy. It lifts the spirits of everyone present. There's no doubt that a good attitude gets things going better sooner. And since your attitude is contagious, it's important to make sure yours is worth catching.

Attitude is one of those little things that makes a big difference. Zig Ziglar says, "It's your attitude, not your aptitude that determines your altitude."

So now we sail on "Attitude" and the more we do, the better our attitude is. We get great ideas while we're out on the water, and it's just plain fun.

I'm proud of our little yacht and I like her name. She's got attitude.

66. The Principle of Vacuum

Nature abhors a vacuum. And so it is with our lives. Everyone is busy—everyone. Ask any retired people you know, and they'll tell you they don't know where the time goes. Their life is full. And they're *retired*.

You can't put any more into a full cup. And when our *lives* are filled to the brim, there's no room for anything else to come in.

As our lives become more and more frenetic, we often become stressed, our health suffers, we have less fun, and we feel more and more powerless. Our lives may feel out of control.

I think the idea of controlling time is a myth. There's no way to control time. All we can do is attempt to control *events*—and even many of *them* are out of our control.

What we need to do is take charge of the things over which we *do* have control. This takes discipline. And it's not easy. With a finite amount of time available to us, we need to choose very carefully. This is our *life*. It's not a dress rehearsal.

The same virtue of which we may be proud—that of sticking to something we've started—*can* work against us. Just because we elected to take something on doesn't mean we have to do it forever. We can make new choices, negotiate new agreements and still maintain our integrity.

In order to make room for what we want, we need to get rid of what we *don't* want. This is the principle of vacuum. Our lives fill up by choice or by default. And we need to choose. This requires a ruthless evaluation of everything we do and why we do it. We can make more time for ourselves by delegating, reducing or eliminating things we're now doing that we either don't like or which don't provide the payoff we want.

Wayne Dyer says relationships that operate from obligation lack integrity. I agree. Your relationship with yourself and with others should be ones of integrity. We want to eliminate the feeling of obligation. This is being truly responsible.

Create some vacuum in your life. Make some room and watch new and better things flow in.

Look for at least three things you're now doing that you'll stop doing or delegate to someone else. Think of how you'd feel if you were no longer obligated to do these things. If it's one of relief, then that's one to go for.

It may not seem immediately apparent what or how something can be eliminated, but it can be done. Start with making a list of everything you do that you don't like doing and everything that no longer has real value to you. Don't let the thought of, "But I have to do this," get in the way of making the list. Figuring out how you'll get it handled is another step. Simply make the list and be honest.

Once you've made the list of hate-to-do's and non- or low-payoff tasks, it's time to start prioritizing. One way is to think about what you'd do if you became incapacitated. How would these things get done? *Would* they get done? What would happen if they didn't? Who else might do it? Be sure to ask yourself what you're getting out of it, and compare it to other things you could be doing that would produce more or better results.

"Money never made a man happy yet, nor will it. The more a man has, the more he wants. Instead of filling a vacuum, it makes one."

—Benjamin Franklin

"Softly and kindly remind yourself, 'I cannot own anything.' It is a valuable thought to keep in mind as you struggle to improve your financial picture, worry about investments, and plan how to acquire more and more. It is a universal principle which you are part of. You must release everything when you truly awaken. Are you letting your life go by in frustration and worry over not having enough? If so, relax and remember that you only get what you have for a short period of time. When you awaken you will see the folly of being attached to anything."

—Wayne Dyer

67. Ten Ways to Exploit the Roaring 2000s

"Tighten your seatbelts and prepare for the greatest boom in history 1998-2008."

Harry S. Dent, Jr.,
author of "The Great Boom Ahead"
and "The Roaring 2000s"

As the number of self-made millionaires in the US increases at the rate of one every 14 minutes and with the average American having a net worth of less than $15,000, one is wise to consider the question: How can I capitalize on the wealth that's being created all around me? How can I position myself and take advantage of the Great Boom in which we are now engaged?

When your children and grandchildren ask about the great prosperity of the early 2000s, what will you tell them? Will you be explaining how you positioned yourself and benefited from the opportunity or will you be justifying how you missed it?

I believe that the predictions of the boom times ahead are accurate. I also want you and me to participate in it. What follows (in no order of importance) are my top ten strategies for exploiting the Roaring 2000s:

1. **Get out of debt.** The quicker the better. You can't take advantage of opportunities when you're mired in debt. You need an attitude and a confidence that comes from being on top of your finances. The chance to buy comes only when you have the resources (however small) to invest in those prospects. Reduce expenses, increase income, negotiate your interest rates, and cut your taxes.

2. **Invest in the wave.** Dent predicts a DOW of over 21,000 and possibly 35,000 by 2008. This is the time to take all cash resources available to get in on this explosion. Buy and buy consistently.

3. **Be flexible.** Things are moving at a rapid pace. This demands adaptability. Things will not remain the same nor will they go back to the way they used to be. Changes that used to evolve over decades or even centuries are happening in years—even months. Entire industries emerge and die within ten years. We must be willing to change directions quickly. It's dodge- and-weave time.

4. **Become techno-savvy.** As of January 2000, over half of all Americans use the Internet. This technology will become more a part of our lives than was ever thought possible. Take a course, get a coach, teach yourself. Whatever you do, get up to speed on using a computer and making the Net work for you.

5. **Be inquisitive.** Constantly ask yourself, "How does this affect me and my industry?" There's no time to sit by and watch things happen. We must be proactive. Talk with people about what's happening. Read. Study. Ask questions.

6. **Think globally.** No longer can we afford to think and act locally. We must have a broader vision. We must think about how our vocation, our business and our industry will operate in a global economy—because it does or soon will.

7. **Be entrepreneurial.** This is the age of the free agent. Even if we are and plan to continue working in a company or organization, we must at least *think* like an entrepreneur. We need to be *in*trepreneurs. Seniority and experience don't have the value that they did. Producing results—and profits—is what matters.

8. **Learn how to learn.** What we learned in high school and college will not support us over the next decade. We must learn how to obtain and integrate information and skills quickly. Computer-based and web-based training will abound. What do you need to learn now? Where and how quickly can you gain the knowledge or skills?

9. **Embrace change.** Be open to the dramatic changes that are occurring. Saying it shouldn't be or making judgments about what's happening is counterproductive. Open yourself to enjoying change. As the Zen Buddhists say, "When you're falling off a cliff, jump."

10. **Become a capitalist.** Wealthy people own assets, other people own liabilities—things that cost money to own and maintain. Capitalism is not a dirty word. A capitalist, by definition, is someone who owns assets—assets that produce income. Stock, equipment and businesses are assets that generate profits. Eighty percent of all millionaires living in America are self-made. Be one of them.

68. Business is All About Relationship

"If humanity does not opt for integrity we are through completely. It is absolutely touch and go. Each one of us could make the difference."

—Buckminster Fuller

I live in a small metropolitan area with only about 110,000 people. And it seems even smaller than that.

I've been doing business in this community for over 20 years. I've worked in non-profits, sales, publishing, printing, construction and now Internet publishing.

Very little of my business is now local. But I often run into people from previous business relationships. Like me, many of these people are in different businesses—often different careers altogether.

It struck me how much my present business relationships have to do with my previous ones. I've found it easy to recreate rapport and establish trust with folks I've had good dealings with before. When I know someone and have confidence in their word, doing business with them becomes easier.

I just had lunch with someone whom I've known and worked with since 1983. All of our dealings have not been positive. In fact, he was hurt financially by some poor business decisions I made in the early 90s. Even so, our friendship weathered that storm because of the depth of the relationship.

I've not always been successful, but I strive to have an excellent relationship with everyone. It doesn't seem possible all the time, but it's worth striving for nonetheless.

Marketing gurus recommend that we be mindful of the lifetime value of a customer—to look not only at the profit from the initial sale. It's good advice, and I would take it a step further: Be mindful of the lifetime value of a *relationship*—not just a customer.

Business is really a network of communication against a background of relationships. And it's not just relationships with customers—it's with suppliers, coworkers, stakeholders—even competitors.

As some of my recent encounters have pointed out, some relationships are completely reversed from what they used to be. Customers can now be employers. Competitors can now be customers. Coworkers may now be bosses.

Today, with the Internet, our business world becomes even smaller. We do business with people around the world, but it's really still a very small community. As I talk with other entrepreneurs online, we seem to know many of the same people.

In a few years, we may each be doing something a bit different. And the relationships we have and build today will serve us in the future in direct proportion to the quality and integrity we create.

 It's important you cultivate and nurture your relationships. Being honest, playing win-win and treating people fairly isn't just a moral thing to do—it's good business—now and in the future.

"Assumptions are the termites of relationships."

—Henry Winkler

"Business is not just doing deals; business is having great products, doing great engineering, and providing tremendous service to customers. Finally, business is a cobweb of human relationships."

—H. Ross Perot

69. The Rule of Three

The United States Marine Corps believes strongly in what they call "The Rule of Three." They've found that implementing this rule saves lives, gets more done faster and more efficiently.

An article on The Corps in *Inc.* magazine says, "The rule dictates that a person should limit his or her attention to three tasks or goals. When applied to strategizing, the rule prescribes boiling a world of infinite possibilities down to three alternative courses of action. Anything more and a Marine can become overextended and confused. The Marines experimented with a rule of four and found that effectiveness plummeted."

I've always believed that three is a powerful number. We find it in some very significant places. The most powerful physical structure is a triangle or pyramid. In fact, it's the building block of Buckminster Fuller's geodesic domes and the Great Pyramids of Egypt. For Christians—it's the Trinity: Father, Son and Holy Spirit. And then, of course, we have Mind, Body, Spirit. Three is a powerful number metaphysically—a number of completion.

As we become immersed in the ocean of information, possibilities, directions and the like, it becomes even more important for us to focus on the things that are truly important to us—the things that will make a difference in the quality of our lives.

Three things can easily be remembered. Any more than that and retention suffers. We can all sharpen our focus and get better results by using the Rule of Three in our daily lives.

Here Are a Few Ideas
List the three most important values in your life. What's really important to you? If you make this list, you'll place yourself in the top one percent of all the people on the planet because very few ever do this. Your decisions will become infinitely easier because your values are clear.

What are your three primary missions? These are different than goals. Goals can be measured. They can be completed. A mission is your vision of something you'll never say is done—at least not in this lifetime.

 Make a list of your three most important goals. It's great to have lots of goals, but which ones are worthy of your best attention and efforts? Remember, you can have *anything* you want in your life. You just can't have *everything* you want.

What three things would you like to master? Three things at which you want to become an expert. Maybe it's speaking in public. Perhaps you want to learn another language. Or maybe you want to become a masterful parent. It's your life and you get to decide.

By making good use of the Rule of Three, you'll sharpen your focus, increase your effectiveness and experience greater fulfillment in all that you do.

"You can do only one thing at a time. I simply tackle one problem and concentrate all efforts on what I am doing at the moment."

— Maxwell Maltz

"The first rule of focus is this: "Wherever you are, be there."

—unknown

"The immature mind hops from one thing to another; the mature mind seeks to follow through."

—Harry A. Overstreet

"You must remain focused on your journey to greatness."

—Les Brown

70. Ten Things to Think About If You Want to Change the World

Mahatma Gandhi believed we must be the change we want to see in the world. This was well demonstrated when he helped India gain its independence from Great Britain. Gandhi was a revolutionary man, but he accomplished India's emergence as a nation without starting a revolution. In fact, he advocated no violence. One of the most powerful countries in the world yielded to the commitment of one man and the dream of millions.

What change can we effect? What's the difference we want to make in the world?

Gandhi said, "In a gentle way you can shake the world." Here are some things to think about how to do just that.

1. **Know that all significant change throughout history has occurred not because of nations, armies, governments—and certainly not committees.** They happened as a result of the courage and commitment of individuals. People like Joan of Ark, Albert Einstein, Clara Barton, Abraham Lincoln, Thomas Edison and Rosa Parks. They might not have done it alone, but they were, without question, the change makers.

2. **Believe you have a unique purpose and potential in the world.** It's not so much something to create as to be discovered. And it's up to you to discover it. Believe you can and will make a difference.

3. **Recognize that everything you do, every step you take, every sentence you write, every word you speak—or *don't* speak—counts.** Nothing is trivial. The world may be big, but there are no small things. Everything matters.

4. **To be the change you want to see in the world, you don't have to be loud.** You don't have to be eloquent. You don't have to be elected. You don't even have to be particularly smart or well educated. You do, however, have to be committed.

5. **Take personal responsibility.** Never think "it's not my job." It's a cop-out to say, "What can I do, I'm only one person." You don't need everyone's cooperation or anyone's permission to make changes. Remember this little gem, "If it's to be, it's up to me."

6. **Don't get caught up in the *how* of things.** If you're clear on what you want to change and why you want to change it, the

how will come. Many significant things have been left undone because someone let the problem solving interfere with the decision making.

7. **Don't wait for things to be just right in order to begin.** Change is messy. Things will never be just right. Follow Teddy Roosevelt's timeless advice, "Do what you can, with what you have, where you are."

8. **The genesis for change is awareness.** We cannot change what we don't acknowledge. Most of the time, we aren't aware of what's wrong or what's not working. We don't see what could be. By becoming more aware, we begin the process of change.

9. **Take to heart these words from Albert Einstein**—arguably one of the smartest change masters who ever lived: "All meaningful and lasting change starts first in your imagination and then works its way out. Imagination is more important than knowledge."

10. **In order for things to change, *you* have to change.** We can't change others; we can only change ourselves. However, when *we* change, it changes everything. And in doing so, we truly can be the change we want to see in the world.

Inscribed on the tomb of an Anglican Bishop in Westminster Abby:

> *"When I was young and free and my imagination had no limits, I dreamed of changing the world. As I grew older and wiser, I discovered the world would not change, so I shortened my sights somewhat and decided to change only my country.*
>
> *But it, too, seemed immovable.*
>
> *As I grew into my twilight years, in one last desperate attempt, I settled for changing only my family, those closest to me, but alas, they would have none of it.*
>
> *And now, as I lie on my deathbed, I suddenly realize: If I had only changed myself first, then by example I would have changed my family.*
>
> *From their inspiration and encouragement, I would then have been able to better my country, and who knows, I may have even changed the world."*

71. What Happens When We Don't Make It?

"An oak tree is just a little nut that held its ground."

We all like to read about successes. We're encouraged by the achievement of others and inspired to hear about how they overcame difficult odds.

But what happens when things don't go as planned? What happens when we just don't make it?

Successful people don't reach all their goals. In fact, they usually miss more than they make.

The fear of missing the mark is one of the reasons we don't set some goals in the first place. We don't want to fall short, and we don't want anyone to know we didn't make it. We don't want to fail.

I'd like to share some thoughts about a goal I didn't reach.

My goal at the beginning of the year was to lose 32 pounds by May 21st. I lost only 14.

There are many other goals over the past few months that *were* met—and even exceeded—but this one was one of the most important. It was also one over which I had the greatest control. It is I and I alone who determines what goes into my mouth and how often and how much I exercise.

It was a doable and believable goal. I had a target date. I had a workable plan and it was a worthy goal.

So what happened?

There were a number of factors that contributed to coming up short, and I'm still evaluating them.

The important thing to realize, however, is that I didn't actually fail. What happened was I missed my target date.

Am I discouraged? A little. Am I disappointed? Yes.

But I can't change what is. I have to survey the results, the *lack* of results and look closely at my plan and how I'll improve upon it.

Am I still committed to it? Yes, indeed. Am I resetting a target date? You bet.

And that's what's important—not giving up.

Until I realized that I had missed the target date instead of failed in the process of achieving my goal, I *was* discouraged. I was focusing on failure instead of the progress I'd made.

The truth is, I'm stronger and healthier now than I was in January. Losing 14 pounds isn't bad. It's not great, but it's better than being where I was, or worse—*gaining* weight.

I get letters all the time from people disheartened because they're not making the progress they think they should. They're discouraged because they didn't succeed. The truth is, achieving big goals is rarely easy.

What *is* easy is to focus on our shortfalls. It's easy to talk to ourselves in negative, counterproductive language: "I'll never make it." "I just can't get it right." "Why don't I ever win?"

Perhaps we're deceived by stories of "overnight" successes. We don't see the setbacks and obstacles that were part of the success. But perseverance almost always wins out. I'm reminded that an oak tree is just a little nut that held its ground.

If it were easy, we wouldn't have the satisfaction that comes with the winning. If we didn't have to change in order to reach the goal, we wouldn't grow. The pain of discipline is only temporary. The glory of achievement lasts much longer.

I'm going to hang in there. I'm going to start over. And I'm going to do it.

 How about you? Do you let the fear of "failure" keep you from setting big goals? Will you keep on keeping on? What goal do you have that needs a recommitment? What will you overcome in order to achieve it? How are you willing to change?

———————

"The pain of discipline is only temporary. The glory of achievement lasts much longer."

—Michael Angier

72. Authenticity and Originality

Why do *real* political leaders seem in such short supply?

Politicians have at their disposal an abundance of opinion polls. Instead of someone who aspires to high office speaking his or her own mind, they speak what they think is the mind of the voters. They want to be sure their position is politically popular or at least not politically *un*popular.

In days of old, there were no speechwriters—our leaders wrote their own. You could pretty much count on what someone was saying as being their own beliefs. Now, you never know if what a speaker is saying is their own or some clever words crafted by a witty speechwriter.

It's extremely rare to find someone willing to share his or her own thoughts or who has much to offer in the way of original thinking. Most of today's so-called leaders lack authenticity, and people sense it.

Winston Churchill once said, "The people cannot look up to a leader who has his ear to the ground." Leaders by definition should *lead* not follow.

Originality and individuality are two of the hallmarks of true leadership. We don't have to agree with someone in order to respect them as a leader. If they feel strongly about something, and we get they truly believe in what they're saying, we ought to at least listen and consider what they have to say.

When someone's telling the truth—speaking from the heart with strong feeling—it's almost impossible to be bored.

There's a Bible phrase I've found easy to remember: "Be hot or cold, but if you be lukewarm, I will spew thee out of my mouth."

Strong words, indeed. What I get from it is, be one way or the other. Being middle-of-the-road doesn't work. The guy who gets my attention is the one who feels strongly about something. The one who has an original approach has the makings of a leader.

When we mouth the words of someone else or speak what we think others want to hear, we relinquish our power. We just add more noise to the world. When we speak from the heart with strong feeling and our own thinking, we stand out from the crowd.

Think of the art world. Which has more value, the original painting or the reproduction? The original, of course.

Reproductions don't even come close to equaling the value of the original. There can only be one original painting and there is only one original you. It's up to each of us to uncover and develop our originality and uniqueness. In doing so, we have more to offer.

Our society tends to promote sameness and commonness. Our schools do their best to make us conform and become more and more like the others. The free spirit is often ostracized. Our employers and our coworkers don't encourage our being different. Often, our attempt to be humble actually thwarts our specialness. And yet almost everything in us cries out to be different and special.

The word "original" comes from the root word origin. And origin is the thing from which anything comes, the starting point or source. Thus, cultivating our originality is only a matter of going back to whence we came—our spirit or God-force.

We may all come from the same source, but we all express our originality in different ways. It's up to us to discover our own uniqueness or own inner splendor. Only in doing so will we actualize our true potential and affect our purpose in the world.

⸻✦⸻

"Men often applaud an imitation and hiss the real thing."

—Aesop

"We need to find the courage to say no to the things and people that are not serving us if we want to rediscover ourselves and live our lives with authenticity."

—Barbara De Angelis

73. There Are No Small Things

In an episode of the TV show, *Unsolved Mysteries*, there was a story of a victim of the holocaust. He'd been placed in a work camp for several years and somehow had managed to survive the horror of his imprisonment.

The story was of a boy—now in his sixties—and his quest to find an American GI who had imparted a kindness to him. The soldier had given the boy some food.

It might seem insignificant, but to this child, who had seen nothing but cruelty and inhumanity for as long as he could remember, it was a gesture that marked a turning point in his life.

When he was liberated by the American forces, he was dying. He needed food. As he was hobbling along the road, a young GI jumped down from his tank and offered him some of his rations.

Unbeknownst to the soldier, the boy had lost hope. He was afraid. He didn't beg for food because he couldn't even conceive the idea that someone would give him some.

With this one act of generosity, a kind and magnanimous American had rekindled a belief that there really was some good in the world.

And the boy never forgot it.

The boy later went to America, raised a family, became successful and worked hard to repay the kindness he had received with kindnesses of his own.

Now, he wanted to find the man who had, in his words, "Saved my life."

I hope he found him. But I'd like to believe there were so many similar acts of generosity that it would be almost impossible to know for sure who the soldier was.

You see, we never know when something we say or do will have a profound influence on another's life.

It's common to think we can't make a difference. And it's sad that most people don't ever recognize what an important role they play—or *could* play. Unlike George Bailey in "It's a Wonderful Life," most of us never get to see how things would be if we weren't here doing what we do.

When I speak to groups, I'm aware of the potential challenges my listeners may be facing. You never know what someone is going through. It might be a divorce. They may have just learned a loved one is dying. They may be afraid of losing their job. Perhaps they don't even *have* a job.

I must be mindful that a thoughtless comment or playful tease could, in fact, be hurtful. We all have a choice: to create more light or to generate more heat in the world. As Confucius put it over 2500 years ago, "It is better to light one small candle than to curse the darkness."

As the story above so nicely illustrates, small gestures can often generate huge blessings. If we're constantly looking for and doing kind and thoughtful acts, we'll no doubt bring more joy into the world around us as well as into our own world.

It's the Law of Reciprocity: the more you do to enhance the lives of others, the more you enhance your own being. It's one of life's better deals.

Robert Brault may have said it best when he wrote, "Enjoy the little things for one day you may look back and realize that they were the big things."

 What kindness can you show today? What generous act can you perform? What kind words will you offer someone? What good deed are you willing to invest in the world?

Do some small things today, but do them in great ways, and you'll assuredly create great blessings.

"Sometimes when I consider what tremendous consequences come from little things . . . I am tempted to think there are no little things."

—Bruce Barton

"A man has made at least a start on discovering the meaning of human life when he plants shade trees under which he knows full well he will never sit."

—D. Elton Trueblood

74. Building Solid Foundations

When it comes to erecting a building, few people would dispute the importance of establishing a strong foundation. And it's no different in building a business, a family or a life.

In 2000, we watched many of the dot-coms become dot-*gones*. One of the reasons for this is that these companies were built without solid foundations.

The emphasis today is on instant gratification. But if we want to build something of value, something that will last, we must build a foundation that will support our vision.

The quick fix, the quick buck and the quick solution will not endure. The individual who shoots to the top of his or her field only to self-destruct is often the victim of not having solidified the values and the structure to support the stardom. It takes effort and it takes conviction, but the rewards are worth it.

Keep Your Eyes on What You're Building

There was once a man passing by a construction site. He stopped and asked one of the tradesmen what he was doing. The worker replied gruffly, "I'm laying bricks, can't you see that?" The man watched a while longer and then asked another worker what he was doing. "I'm just earning a living," he replied. A third time the man asked a worker and the response was much different, "I'm building a cathedral."

No doubt the personal happiness and the quality of the work from the last man was much better than from the first two.

And what about us? Are we just collecting a paycheck, doing drudgery work—laying bricks? Or are we building a cathedral?

By staying focused on what we're building and seeing the task at hand as accomplishing that purpose, we'll gain greater satisfaction, our work will be lighter, and we'll create more excellence.

Foundations Take Time

I recently watched a building being constructed. (I must admit I was tempted to ask some of the workers what they were doing.) For months, there seemed to be little progress. There was plenty of dust, lots of activity, but very little evidence that anything was really happening.

That's because they were building the foundation—the foundation to support a grand structure. And that takes time.

The engineers, the architect and the owner certainly weren't standing around saying, "Where's the building? Why can't I see more progress?" They knew that a majority of the time required to construct the building would be spent in laying the groundwork.

Once the foundation is ready and cured, the rest of the construction happens at an impressive speed. Even mistakes made in the superstructure can be corrected without too much difficulty. But faults in the foundation *cannot* be easily repaired and will jeopardize the entire structure.

And why should what we build be any different? We need to put strong foundations under our dreams, our businesses and our relationships. I believe this is where many people struggle. They're too focused on the payoff and don't give enough attention to the hard work and careful planning required in building the substructure. They want to start putting up walls and bringing in the business too soon.

And in the end, most fail because there's not the right support.

Every business, every marriage, every cause will be tested. Just being a "good guy" and "doing the right thing" will not insulate you from the gales, the attacks and the infestations that will most definitely occur.

But with a strong foundation, built with good materials, with painstaking effort, your structure will be one that withstands all assaults and fully supports your endeavors.

"A successful man is one who can lay a firm foundation with the bricks others have thrown at him."

—David Brinkley

"I respect the man who knows distinctly what he wishes. The greater part of all mischief in the world arises from the fact that men do not sufficiently understand their own aims. They have undertaken to build a tower, and spend no more labor on the foundation than would be necessary to erect a hut."

—Johann Wolfgang von Goethe

75. Truth or Consequences

When I was seven, I moved for a brief time to Columbus, Georgia with my family while my father went on active duty for the Army. I was a new kid in a new school and wanted to make friends quickly.

One day in music class, the teacher asked if any of us knew how to play the piano. Eager to make an impression, I volunteered that I had learned on my grandmother's piano. The only part of this that was true was that my grandmother *owned* a piano. I thought if everyone believed I was so talented, it would help earn their respect and admiration.

When our teacher asked me to come forward and play something, I knew I was in big trouble. Up until that point, I had never known how entertaining the truth could be. Kids just love seeing someone make a complete fool of themselves.

Telling the truth is not always easy. Lying is. And yet I've never seen, where in the long run, telling a lie has proven useful. If one truly wishes to live a successful life, honesty is not only the best policy, it's the *only* policy.

Being truthful might not be easy, but it is simple. When faced with a question, we have three choices: we can tell the truth, we can lie, or we can refuse to answer the question.

For those of us striving to lead lives of personal and professional excellence, we must look carefully at how we operate. Do we tell the truth? Always?

Under what circumstances do we feel justified in telling less than the truth? Does it ever pay off positively? Where and when do we lie to ourselves? Do we live our lives in a manner whereby we're never tempted to lie or cover up our actions? For me, it's a constant examination. And I continue to find areas where I'm less than forthright—especially with myself.

It's been almost fifty years since that humbling experience in my second-grade music class. I'd like to say I learned my lesson once and for all; that I never again misrepresented the truth. But that wouldn't *be* the truth. I've managed to blow it many times since—although never quite so embarrassingly.

Sir Walter Scott knew the wisdom of truth-telling when he wrote, "Oh what a tangled web we weave when first we practice to deceive."

At no time in history has it been harder to lie and get away with it. The information age has made it likely that the truth will at some point be exposed.

Bet on the truth. Six-and-a-half-thousand years of recorded history have given us story after story proving that nothing justifies nor warrants lying—nothing.

"Truth is generally the best vindication against slander."

—Abraham Lincoln

"I have been truthful all along the way. The truth is more interesting, and if you tell the truth you never have to cover your tracks."

—Real Live Preacher

"Whoever is careless with the truth in small matters cannot be trusted with important matters."

—Albert Einstein

"Always tell the truth—it's the easiest thing to remember."

—David Mamet

"Even if you are a minority of one, the truth is the truth."

—Mahatma Gandhi

"If you do not tell the truth about yourself you cannot tell it about other people."

—Virginia Woolf

76. Change Happens: How to Accept, Navigate and Master Change

Not only do we live in a time of unprecedented change, but the changes we're experiencing are happening at a faster and faster rate. The telephone, radio and TV took decades to be placed into common use. Now the time it takes from invention to widespread usage is just a few years—sometimes months!

Most of the change we're experiencing is appreciated. We like most of what we see happening. While we enjoy many of these changes, there are other changes that are not so warmly embraced. There's more uncertainty, less confidence and—as a result—more stress.

I'm a recreational sailor. There's hardly anything I enjoy more than being out on the water with the wind in my sails. Sailing has taught me many things—not the least of which is a healthy respect for the wind. You have absolutely no control over the wind—only the way you use it. You must master your ability to handle the wind, regardless how hard it blows or from which direction it blows.

And change is like the wind. It's neither good nor bad. It just is.

How we feel about change—our attitudes toward it—will have much to do with how well we navigate this turbulent sea of change. If we dislike change, resist it, ignore it or resent it, we'll lose.

On the other hand, if we use it to our advantage, we'll benefit from it.

Choice or No Choice
If the new situation is to your liking or a result of your own choosing, you'll likely have a different reaction than if the change seems forced upon you—a new responsibility at work, a shopping mall going in next door or your spouse telling you they want a divorce.

Recognize Change
You can't change what you don't acknowledge. Oftentimes we're slow to realize or even fail to recognize changes that occur. We need to look at what's happening and acknowledge what we need to change in ourselves in order to adapt to the changes around us.

Which brings us to one of the first steps in dealing with change . . .

How Will this Change Affect Me?

Too often, people resist change before allowing themselves to explore its potential benefits.

Make a sincere effort to look for the good in what appears to be changing. Because of a natural resistance to the unknown, you must consciously and logically analyze what this difference will mean to you. And it's often not what you first perceive.

How Can I Exploit this Change?

Many fortunes have been made by taking swift advantage of changes and trends before others have realized how to do so.

A change that alters the rules is an opportunity only if you're able to see the new connections—and exploit them.

If after thoroughly exploring the potential good, you see the change as negatively impacting you, then ask the next question . . .

Is There Anything I Can Do About this?

There's no question that some change runs counter to your best interests. If this is the case, you need to find out if you can change the circumstances. This is no time to play victim. Often what *looks* like a situation totally outside of your control can in fact be altered.

If you can't change the circumstances, then ask . . .

How Can I Minimize the Impact of this Change?

First, accept it. There's no payoff to being upset about it. If your destination is Los Angeles and you find yourself in San Francisco due to bad weather or mechanical difficulties, being angry about it will not get you to Los Angeles. In fact it will hinder you.

Your success is largely dependent upon your acceptance and response to the change that takes place around you. Extinctions occur as a result of an inability to change. To change is often difficult, but to not change may prove fatal.

Those who will thrive in this new millennium will be those who have positive attitudes toward change. Those who don't will be left behind, or worse yet, they will founder.

 What's your attitude toward change? What are your beliefs about the change you see around you and the change that surely lies ahead? When faced with something new and different, do you long for the old way or do you look for what advantages this may bring to you, your family, your business.

77. Your Market Value

You don't get paid for your time. You get paid for the value you bring to the marketplace.

How much value are you creating? And are you getting paid for it?

My wife and I have had some discussions lately about how to charge for our time and services. Like many people, we have a tendency to undervalue what we have to offer.

The good news is we each see the other as having more value than we see for ourselves, and this has helped our pricing strategy immensely.

I charge four to five times as much for my time now as I did only a few years ago. Am I worth four to five times more now? Possibly, but I rather think my own perception of what my time is worth has tripled. That, and the positive feedback that comes from people quickly saying "yes" when you tell them your rates.

It's not just the value of time, either. I've actually seen price tests on new products where a higher price outsold (in units) the lower price of the same product. When it comes to the marketplace, perception is the only reality.

What determines our value? (By the way, I'm speaking only in terms of our market or economic value here.) We are each incredibly valuable—make that priceless—people.

Market value is based on the age-old law of supply and demand. It's determined by:

1. The demand for the type of work you do

2. How well you do what you do

3. How difficult it would be to replace you

4. The demand for you exclusively

Why do some brain surgeons make more performing one operation than another person earns in a year? Because they score highly in all four of the above criteria.

The salaries and contracts of many of the top professional athletes today may seem crazy, but notice how they match up to this list.

Think about these things and look for ways to enhance your income by positioning yourself well in all four areas.

"When it becomes more difficult to suffer than change, you will change."

—unknown

"He who moves not forward, goes backward."

—Johann Wolfgang von Goethe

"When you're a beautiful person on the inside, there is nothing in the world that can change that about you. Jealousy is the result of one's lack of self-confidence, self-worth, and self-acceptance. The Lesson: If you can't accept yourself, then certainly no one else will."

—Sasha Azevedo

78. The Four Stages of Learning

Paul Zane Pilzer, a leading economist, predicts that nearly half of the jobs people will have in the next five years haven't even been invented yet. Today, over 90% of the jobs in the U.S. weren't in existence when most of us were born.

What that tells me is that understanding the learning process is a major key to our future success. There are four stages of learning anything.

1. **Unconscious Incompetence**
   This is when you don't *know* that you don't know how to do something. For instance, a young child isn't aware that he doesn't know how to drive a car.

2. **Conscious Incompetence**
   In the second stage, you become aware you don't know how to do something. You *know* that you don't know. This awareness is critical. Attempting to drive a car without knowing *how* to drive a car could prove fatal.

3. **Conscious Competence**
   The third stage is when we know how to do something, but it requires we be very much aware of what we're doing.

   To continue with our example, when you first learn how to drive a car, you must concentrate on blending the power, easing out the clutch, watching traffic and the many other skills that are part of operating an automobile.

4. **Unconscious Competence**
   This is when you've reached a level of competency, which requires little or no thought. The skills are ingrained so deeply that you can talk, adjust the radio, open the window and think about your next presentation—all while orchestrating the direction, speed and performance of the car.

As we progress through the new millennium, being able to learn new skills and quickly access information will be critical to our success. Knowing *how* to learn will become one of our greatest assets.

79. Simplifying Our Life: We Wanted to Before—Now We Will!

Dawn and I—and our cat Rex—plan to give up our condo in The Green Mountain State and head out on the road for a couple of years. Our home will be a "diesel pusher" motor coach, and we'll follow the thermometer around North America

As you can imagine, this marks a major change in our life and to our lifestyle. And we have a lot to do to make it happen. Finances, logistics, plans and contingencies must all be handled.

One of the things we have to do is something we've always tried to do, but never did as well as we would have liked—simplify our lives. Our plans provide new impetus to get serious about doing just that. We'll rid ourselves of all unnecessary possessions and set up our affairs so we can easily operate from wherever we are.

It's not that we need it, but this new chapter in our lives will certainly feel like a fresh start. We're looking forward to it, and we'll report from the road on our experiences.

We'll digitize as much of our business as we possibly can. We'll arrange for automatic bill payments and do all of our banking online.

And we'll sell or give away almost everything we own. Only a few items will be placed in storage. Living in a 40-foot motor coach will force us to keep only what we absolutely need.

Most of us accumulate too much "stuff" in our lives. I've often thought it would be worth it to move every few years just to sort out what we really want to keep. And even that doesn't always work.

 You don't have to go on the road to simplify your life. Start brainstorming how you can simplify your life. What do you have that no longer serves you? What can you get rid of? Remember, everything you own owns a little bit of you. It has to be cleaned, repaired, insured and stored. One of the ways to make room for what you *do* want is to get rid of what you *don't* want.

Clean out the garage, the attic, the basement—the entire house or office. Have a garage sale. Give things to the Salvation Army or your local thrift store. Feel the freedom that comes from clearing the decks.

80. You Never Know When Your Words Will Make a Difference

"Praise, like gold and diamonds,
owes its value to its scarcity."

—Samuel Johnson

In his autobiography, *My American Journey*, Colin L. Powell tells of an experience he had when he was a colonel in Korea.

Powell had worked hard to carry out the wishes of his commanding officer. It was not an order with which he agreed. It was an attempt to impress a visiting dignitary, and he felt it was a waste of time and energy for his men. Nevertheless, he dutifully accomplished the assignment.

When the ordeal was finished, Powell felt like a fraud. With his head drooping, he was visibly embarrassed. A first sergeant fell into step with him as he walked away. "That was a hoot, sir, wasn't it?"

"It was stupid," Powell blurted out. "I hate to see the troops do stupid things. And I hate to be the one responsible for it."

The sergeant was quiet for a time. "Colonel Powell, don't worry. We don't know what that was all about. But the men know you wouldn't have cooked up something that dumb on your own. They trust you. They won't hold it against you. We went along because you needed it. Relax, sir."

It was this next paragraph in General Powell's story that struck me.

"In all my years in the Army, among all the citations, medals and promotions, I never appreciated any tribute more than I did the sergeant's words at that low point."

Here is one of the most admired and respected men in the world, who was deeply affected by the kind and supportive words of a subordinate. I wouldn't be surprised if that young sergeant doesn't even remember saying what he did to Colin Powell that night.

No doubt there have been people in your life who have said something to you that inspired or encouraged you at an important time.

We all affect everyone else. And we rarely know when it's had an impact on someone. What we say, what we do, and how we are being, can make a profound impression on others.

Constantly look for ways to encourage and support others. Your encouragement will surely make a difference.

Who can you encourage today?

"You have it easily in your power to increase the sum total of this world's happiness now. How? By giving a few words of sincere appreciation to someone who is lonely or discouraged. Perhaps you will forget tomorrow the kind words you say today, but the recipient may cherish them over a lifetime."

—Dale Carnegie

"Those who are lifting the world upward and onward are those who encourage more than criticize."

—Elizabeth Harrison

"Flatter me, and I may not believe you. Criticize me, and I may not like you. Ignore me, and I may not forgive you. Encourage me, and I may not forget you."

—William Arthur

81. Our Self-Esteem

*"Low self-esteem is like driving through
life with your hand-break on."*

— Maxwell Maltz

A reader from the Middle East wrote to me recently asking how he could improve his low self-image. He said, "it ruins my social and professional life." He wanted to know what techniques he could employ to solve this lifelong problem.

I felt somewhat inadequate in my reply to him and resolved to write about my own struggles to improve self-esteem in hopes it will be helpful to others.

I know people who have too much confidence and self-pride, but I don't know *anyone* with too much self-esteem. Most people, in moments of profound honesty, will admit to a lack of self-esteem. They would like to feel better about themselves—more confident and capable. In short, to love themselves more.

It would probably be fair to say most social problems are the result—directly or indirectly—of someone's low self-concept.

Not too many years ago, I was going through a dark time in my life. I was broke—financially, personally and socially. In describing it to someone once, I said, "I had the self-esteem of a dead rat." That might have been overstating it a bit, but not much.

My life—and my confidence—are so much better today. *Much* better.

So what changed? Was it outward circumstances? Did my environment change and with it my inner experience? No.

Somehow I knew that any changes would have to be from me. It would be an inner transformation that would eventually alter the outward experience.

First and foremost, I removed myself from people who had been particularly critical. By distancing myself from this criticism, I was able to gain a better perspective. I was perfectly capable of taking my own inventory and didn't need someone else pointing out my errors and keeping me focused on my shortcomings.

I immersed myself in good books—books of inspiration, books that increased my belief and books that gave me hope. And hope was severely lacking.

I made a conscious attempt to focus on my strengths: my talents, my experience and my knowledge. I didn't allow myself to indulge in negative thoughts. When I found myself musing about something less than "uplifting," I would redirect myself to something else. I gave myself no permission to have "pity parties."

I took to heart Thomas Carlyle's advice when he wrote, "Our main business is not to see what lies dimly at a distance, but to do what clearly lies at hand." I kept busy. I did what appeared to me as needing doing. I didn't know exactly what I wanted to do or how I was going to do it. The future was uncertain, and for the first time in my life, I didn't have a plan.

And each day I did what I could to clean up my messes, make things better, keep my focus forward instead of backward and keep the faith.

One of the biggest awarenesses I had during these dark times was that I *was not* my feelings. I *had* feelings, but they were not me. I also realized that I had cared too much about the opinions of others. I still care; I just don't let it run me like it used to.

Some people believe that if you feel good about yourself, you'll do great things. I also believe if you do great things, you'll feel good about yourself—and then do even greater things.

Taking these steps consistently over a period of years has enabled me to rebuild my finances, establish a career I'm excited about, develop a loving and committed marriage and, most importantly, restore and improve upon my self-esteem. I'm grateful for the process.

Self-esteem is an upward or downward spiral. What you do affects the way you feel. How you feel affects the things you do. The things you do affect what you and others think of you, which in turn, affects how you feel about yourself.

You're either building yourself up or tearing yourself down. There is no status quo when it comes to your self-esteem.

"Confidence is contagious. So is lack of confidence."

—Michael O'Brien

82. Celebrate Your Success

"Those at the top of the mountain didn't fall there."

—Marcus Washling

An important element of the science of achievement is the need to celebrate our successes. It's also one that's easily ignored and even contradicted.

The problem for many of us is we never quite feel successful, because as soon as we reach one goal or pass a certain milestone, we're already going after the next one. Too often, we don't stop to revel in the feeling of accomplishment. We're too focused on the next rung of the ladder—that's if we've even noticed we've moved up another rung.

I'm not advocating resting on our laurels. I'm suggesting we truly experience the joy that comes from seeing our progress and accomplishing our objectives.

I recently completed and published a book called, *101 Best Ways to Get Ahead.* It feels great to have it done, and I'm getting lots of accolades from people I respect and admire. It's a good book. An easy read—both entertaining and informative.

But I find it a little too easy for me to look at ways I could have done it better. In doing so, I take away from my satisfaction—my sense of accomplishment and joy.

And I know I'm not alone in this process. The people I interview and coach share that they do the same thing. No job seems good enough. No achievement is great enough.

It's the wrong focus. When we do this, we're being ungrateful—we're thwarting abundance.

We can always see ways we could have done it better or faster. But the truth is we did it. In my case, having published a book is clearly a milestone—something millions of people aspire to and yet only a few thousand actually achieve.

So I'm going to celebrate it. I'm going to indulge myself in feelings of triumph and success, and I'm going to resist the natural tendency to disparage my work or myself.

I keep a *Win List.* I find that listing the wins in my life—big and small—is more than therapeutic. And it's a real pick-me-up to review the good things that have happened to me as well as the things I've made happen.

It keeps me grateful and it keeps me focused on the good stuff.

Celebrating our successes employs a universal law: when we appreciate what we have and what we've done, we find ourselves having more to appreciate.

 What accomplishment can you celebrate? What milestones can you highlight or acknowledge? Your last promotion? Helping someone through a tough time? Winning that new contract? Losing those five pounds? Giving that presentation?

When you do these things, it anchors positive feelings into your consciousness and prepares you for more of the same. Like attracts like and your feelings are powerful magnets indeed.

"Great things are not done by impulse, but by a series of small things brought together."

—Vincent Van Gogh

"What it comes down to is that anybody can win with the best horse. What makes you good is if you can take the second- or third-best horse and win."

—Vicky Aragon

83. Ten Ways to Stay Focused on Your Objectives

People often ask me what I think are the most important keys to achieving successful outcomes. There are many, but the one thing I see as being the most essential—and often ignored—is consistency.

Any worthwhile, challenging goal requires sustained effort. Doing the things necessary for a day or two isn't hard. Where most people fall down is in stringing those days together, creating the progress, the momentum, and ultimately, the successful accomplishment.

What follows are ten ways to maintain your focus, your energy and your optimism while pursuing your goal. They've worked for me and they'll work for you. When I've employed all of these components, I've never failed to achieve my intention.

1. **Have Powerful Reasons.** With a strong enough reason, you can and will find the how and the resources to achieve your reward. Reasons plus belief keep you motivated. When you're excited about your goal, it doesn't seem like work. If you're not excited, your efforts will require more discipline and energy. Make sure it's *your* goal. Make sure it excites you. And then act enthusiastically.

2. **Write Your Objectives Down.** This is a critical step. Don't just *think* it, *ink* it. When you write your goals down, they appear not only on paper, but they become indelibly written upon your consciousness.

3. **Visualize**. "See" your objective already in existence. Nothing can withstand the power of a clear, multi-sensory vision of what you're intending. What does it look like? What will people be saying about it? How will you feel? The more detailed and "real" you can make your vision, the more powerful it will be. It will operate like a magnet and draw forth all kinds of things you never thought possible.

4. **Affirm Your Success.** Speak your goal into existence. An affirmation is a present-tense, positive statement of your intended outcome. I now have achieved _____ (fill in the blank). The more sensory rich you can make your affirmations, the more effective they will be. All of these techniques help you to feel the presence of your objective and build belief.

5. **Make a Plan of Action.** To achieve and stay focused upon your objective, create an action plan. What are the steps you'll take to get you from where you are to where you want to be? Your

strategies will likely change as you go along, so set your goals in concrete and your plans in sand. Keep your eye on the goal, but remain flexible in your path to it.

6. **Measure Your Progress.** It's hard to change what you don't measure. Create mechanisms that will allow you to see your progress. Use charts. Log your actions. Use anything that will encourage you by allowing you to objectively track your progress. We all need feedback—it's the breakfast of champions.

7. **Maintain a Support System.** Have a Master Mind Group. Use the Buddy System. Surround yourself with people who will encourage and challenge you. Announce your intentions. Be accountable to someone other than yourself. Read positive books. Review past successes.

8. **Focus on Only a Few Goals at a Time.** You can achieve anything you desire, but not *everything* you desire. Concentrate your efforts and your energy on just a few. I might have dozens of goals and projects, but I keep three key goals in the forefront of my mind.

9. **Take Action Every Day.** An important objective warrants daily attention. A 400-page novel is not written all at once. To many, writing a 400-page novel would be overwhelming. But a little over a page a day will get it done in a year. Every goal can be broken down into doable tasks done consistently.

10. **Celebrate Your Milestones.** Mark your successes and acknowledge yourself for your progress. As you achieve one goal, you can see better and believe more easily in the accomplishment of others. You deserve to succeed, and you deserve to celebrate your successes.

"Many people flounder about in life because they do not have a purpose, an objective toward which to work."

—George Halas

"To me, the definition of focus is knowing exactly where you want to be today, next week, next month, next year, then never deviating from your plan. Once you can see, touch and feel your objective, all you have to do is pull back and put all your strength behind it, and you'll hit your target every time."

—Bruce Jenner

84. Ten Ways to Support Someone in Being Their Best

One of the greatest responsibilities we have is to support ourselves and others in living at our highest and best. Whether we're parents, partners, friends or leaders, it's incumbent upon us to help others to live as close to their unique potential as we can.

With everything you say and do, you're influencing—positively or negatively—the people you care about. Here are ten ways you can help others see and realize the best that's within them.

1. Believe in Them

We all have self-doubts from time to time. Our confidence is shaken. We lack the faith in our talents and skills to go for an important promotion or launch a new initiative. Having someone believe in you at these times is priceless.

2. Encourage Them

"You can do it." "I know you can." These are words that are all-too-infrequently voiced. Sincere encouragement can go a long way in helping someone stay the course. The more specific you are, the better the results. "I remember when you got through your slump last year and ended up winning the sales contest. I'm willing to bet you'll do even better this time."

3. Expect a Lot

We're often told not to get our hopes up. We're encouraged to have *realistic* expectations. But when it comes to helping others operate at their best, we sometimes have to up-level our expectations. This can be taken to extremes, but there are many times when a teacher, a parent or even a boss has required more of us than we thought we were capable. And we've risen to the challenge which enabled us to see further than before.

4. Tell the Truth

And tell it with compassion. We often avoid telling the hard truth because we don't want to upset anyone. We want to be *nice*. But telling the truth is a loving act. You may be the only person who can or will say to another what needs to be said. And you can confront someone without being combative.

5. Be a Role Model

One of the best ways you influence is by your own actions. Who you are speaks much more loudly than what you say. Don't think that people aren't watching you. They are. And they're registering everything about you consciously and unconsciously. We automatically emulate our role models. And we're *all* role models to someone, so let's be good ones.

6. **Share Yourself**
Too often, we miss the value of sharing our failings. We don't want to be vulnerable, so we hold back. In doing so, we deprive others of our experience, our learning and our humanity. When you share from your own experience—especially your failures— you increase empathy, you're more approachable and you increase your relatability to others.

7. **Challenge Them**
The word "challenge" has some negative connotations. The meaning we're using here is, "a test of one's abilities or resources in a demanding but stimulating undertaking." We all need to be challenged from time to time. Doing it for another is an art form. Go too far and it will backfire. Go too easy, and you will appear patronizing.

8. **Ask Good Questions**
A good therapist or coach doesn't tell their clients what to do. They ask good questions in order for the client to understand themselves better, to get clear on what the issue is and from there to make better choices. You can do the same. By asking elegant questions, you cause people to think and come up with solutions.

9. **Acknowledge Them**
You find what you're looking for. If you're looking for the best in someone, you'll see it. If you're looking for their failings, you'll see those. Catch people doing things right and tell them. When we acknowledge the good deeds of others, they tend to do more of them. Write a note. Send a card. Give them a call. Praise them in front of others.

10. **Spend Time with Them**
We love what we give our time to. By devoting your most precious resource (time) to another individual, you're showing them you truly value them and your relationship with them. Invest time in your relationships; it's what life is made of.

85. Ten Reasons to Live a Life of Integrity

You might think it's a no-brainer why one should live an honest life. But it's apparent to me that a life of integrity is the exception rather than the rule. How many people do you know who are honest all the time?

We could make a case about the morality and the "rightness" of living honestly. Religious leaders have been advocating this for thousands of years. It's doubtful many of them could provide a true model of integrity.

I believe in the moral and ethical value of integrity, but I also think there are very practical and worthwhile reasons for living an impeccable life. Here are ten:

1. **Trust.** In order to be successful in business or hold a responsible job, a person must have a reputation of honesty. Resources are not entrusted to people who have proven themselves as untrustworthy.

2. **Good Health.** I have no research to support this, but I'd be willing to bet that people who tell the truth are healthier. They have less concern, less stress and feel better about themselves. This has to translate into better health.

3. **Pride.** I've yet to meet a liar who has any real pride in themselves. Any good leadership training will stress the importance and value of having pride in what you do and who you are. If your reputation is grounded in deception, your opinion of yourself is poor indeed. Being honest just plain feels good.

4. **Peace of Mind.** If you cheat on your income taxes, you may get away with it, but you'll probably always worry you'll get audited and face fines, extra charges and even jail as a result. Your reputation would also be tarnished. When you deal honestly, you have peace of mind. It's impossible to worry and be happy at the same time.

5. **Remembering.** It's been said that no one has a good enough memory to be a good liar. When you don't tell the truth, you have to *invent* something. When you do, you'll often be asked to recall what you said, and you may not be able to do so because you forgot. You *know* the truth, but you can't remember your version of it. Very embarrassing. Besides, it's hard work to continually come up with false stories.

6. **Good Sleep.** If you lie—unless you have no conscience at all— you'll often lose sleep because of your fears of being found out. Your worry and your guilt will keep you awake.
   A good night's sleep is one of life's many pleasures and honest people sleep better.

7. **Confidence.** Many people have excellent "bull" detectors. They know—at least at some level—when you're being fake.
   If telling lies is your modus operandi, you know these people will often see though your façade. There's no way to have real confidence in yourself when you're walking on "bull."

8. **Good Relationships.** Relationships are the jewels of our lives. One could argue that relationships *are* our lives. And breeches in trust are the death knell of relationships. When trust is gone, there is no foundation upon which to build. Relationships lacking in trust seem hollow and shallow. They lack joy.

9. **Legal Problems.** We don't have to look very far to see the legal trouble people get themselves into from dishonesty. Lying in a court of law or to an officer of the law is literally *against* the law. Conversely, if you have no secrets, you can rest easy and it's hard for anyone to blackmail you.

10. **It Doesn't Work.** All too often, our deceptions and duplicity are discovered. In the information age in which we live, it's even more likely lies will sooner or later be seen for what they are. Dishonesty is just plain inefficient.

The right thing to do is seldom the easy thing to do. And it's worth it.

"Nothing astonishes men so much as common sense and plain dealing."

—Ralph Waldo Emerson

"The truth is incontrovertible. Malice may attach it. Ignorance may deride it. But in the end, there it is."

—Winston Churchill

86. It's Easy to Lose Credibility

"Business is simple. Make some stuff and sell it for more than it cost you. There's nothing more to it than that except for a few million details."

—president of International Harvester

I had to eat a little humble pie recently. And I want to share why, because I think it illustrates a critical lesson in how easy it can be for clients—or potential clients—to lose confidence in you.

We had asked our readers to complete a short survey to obtain some feedback on the buying process for our new book, *101 Best Ways to Get Ahead from 101 of the World's Most Successful People.*

To reward our respondents for their time, I offered them a free copy of a report that sells for $3.95. We had a great response and a number of people said they really appreciated being given something for their feedback.

But one man pointed something out to me that caused me to wince. When we updated this report a while back, we increased the price from $2.95 to $3.95. I stated in my offer what it sold for by saying, " . . . if you used only a third of the advice in it, it would be worth a hundred times the $3.95." I believe that statement to be true or I wouldn't have said it.

But as it turns out—and as this gentleman politely pointed out—we'd neglected to change the price on the product itself. All references to *101 Best Ways to Save Time* were for $3.95, but the *cover* price on the report itself still said $2.95. When this respondent saw this, he told me our credibility had been diminished.

And he was right.

It doesn't matter that it was unintentional. It doesn't matter that he didn't even pay $3.95. What matters is the perception people have.

It takes a long time to build credibility—and so *little* to degrade or destroy it. It takes only one tiny inconsistency or inaccuracy for people to question everything else you say and do.

We've been in business for almost ten years. We've worked hard to provide services and sell products that deliver what we promise—usually more. We fully and unconditionally guarantee everything we sell. We bend over backward to please our customers, clients and members.

People trust us. We've built a solid reputation, and we're very well respected.

But one can never rest on one's laurels. We have to be diligent and always remember how easily it can be lost—how one transgression will overshadow dozens of good experiences.

I feel fortunate to do business with people I trust and who trust me. What I have to remind myself is that not everyone operates this way and many of you have been burned by less-than-scrupulous transactions.

My learning was a reminder of how fragile trust is. My learning was that I can never take it for granted, and I must be extraordinarily attentive to every detail and how it will be perceived.

 Examine carefully your policies, your practices, your communications—everything you do, and don't do, for inaccuracies, exaggerations and misleading statements.

Guard your reputation and your credibility like it was the most important thing you have. Because it may very well be.

"The more you are willing to accept responsibility for your actions, the more credibility you will have."

—Brian Koslow

87. A $2.4 Million Personality

According to an Associated Press story, the headline above is true.

It seems that Gwen Butler, a bartender in an upscale restaurant in Boston's Beacon Hill section, made quite an impression on one of her patrons—a multimillion-dollar impression.

Gwen is a tall, 29-year-old woman with an infectious smile and a vivid dream—to own her own restaurant. Last February, when she waited on Erich Sager, a Swiss financier, she impressed him with her attention to service, her vivacious personality and her great smile.

They met later to discuss the particulars. He asked how much she would need to do it up right. She said, "at least two million." She and her friend and future business partner, Chris Rapzcynski, wrote up a business plan. In the end, Sager invested $2.4 million.

Several times over the last few years Gwen had been offered backing by customers she had met, but each time it turned out to be just a pickup line or an empty promise. This time it was for real.

The restaurant business has one of the highest failure rates of any industry. So why would a savvy businessman take such a chance? I'm betting it's because he saw in Gwen the kind of person who has what it takes to make a go of it. He caught her dream. Her restaurant is scheduled to open in September.

You never know when an opportunity will present itself. And it's important that we're properly prepared.

What if Gwen had been in a bad mood and let it show that day? What if her dream wasn't alive? What if she hadn't given Erich excellent service? Would she have been able to attract the financing? I think not.

You could say she was lucky—that she was in the right place at the right time. And that's true—she was. But what I've found is that magic happens when a prepared mind and a powerful dream meet opportunity.

At least once a month I ask my thirteen-year-old son to tell me the three rules of life. He usually rolls his eyes but dutifully recites all three: number one, be nice; number two, be nice and number three, yup, be nice.

That's what I think happened in Boston. It sure paid off for Gwen.

88. Getting Back to Basics

Legend has it that the great Green Bay Packer coach, Vince Lombardi, used to start off each training season by sitting his pro football players down and telling them, "Gentlemen, today we're going to get back to the basics of the game. This, (holding the pigskin over his head) is a *football.*"

The coach knew the importance of understanding and reviewing the fundamentals of the sport. And in the complex world in which we live, it's good for *us* to do the same.

What are the basics in *your* life? What's really important to you? And are you truly doing things that support the answers to these questions? Most of us would have to admit we're not doing as well as we'd like.

In any family, any business, any *life*, we find ourselves doing things that no longer serve us—if they ever did in the first place. We start a project, a job or a routine, and we continue doing it because it's become habitual. Even though we've changed and things around us have changed, we continue a practice that may no longer be necessary or even helpful to us.

From time to time, we have to get back to the basics. What do we want? Why do we want it? What are the best ways to get it? Otherwise, we stay busy just doing what we've been doing.

Many people today yearn for a simpler life. That's good. But we have to do more than *yearn* for it; we have to take action. Sometimes we even have to *stop* doing what we're doing, take a good, honest look at where we are, what we're doing and what we're *not* doing.

We have to get back to the basics.

 Examine everything you're doing and why you're doing it. What are you spending money on? Are you still receiving value from those expenditures? Does what you're doing and what you're spending money on match your core values?

Time is our most precious resource. And it's paramount we do things that bring us joy and add to the richness of our lives and the lives of others.

Have a conversation about these ideas with your spouse, partner or coach. Don't go through your days robotically. We are human beings, not human *doings*. Make *choices*—good choices.

89. How Full is Your Cup?

*"Wisdom is meaningless until our own experience
has given it meaning."*

—Bergen Evans

I was trying to counsel a young man the other day who was less than receptive to taking advice. He said he wanted help, but in fact he wanted someone to fix his problems. He said he wanted advice, but instead he wanted to be right.

Isn't it interesting when people have all the answers and no money?

Here was someone who was broke and had no job. His life wasn't working. You'd think he would be willing to learn, but sadly, this was not the case.

I'm reminded of the story of the young mystic who traveled a great distance to study at the feet of a revered sage. When the young man arrived, he proceeded to try and impress the master with how much he knew and how wise he was.

Instead of asking questions, the student went on about his beliefs and philosophies. The master listened quietly for a long while.

Finally, the student stopped talking for a few moments. The master asked his guest if he would like some tea. "Why, yes," the young man replied.

The old man began to pour the tea into his visitor's cup. But he didn't stop when the cup was full. He continued to pour as the tea overflowed into the saucer and then onto the tabletop where it began to run out on the floor.

"Stop!" the young man said. "The cup is full. Can't you see? It can hold no more."

"It's true," the wise one said. "We cannot put more into an already full cup. And you are like that cup. Until you empty yourself of yourself, your fullness will prevent you from learning."

To some extent, we're all a bit like the young man. We sometimes have to let go of what we think we know in order to embrace new ideas.

We're always free to pick up our old beliefs and "knowings" at a later time, but we need to be open in order to look at things in a new way. We need to approach knowledge with the wonder and openness of a child. This way, we keep from missing important lessons and learning helpful life strategies.

It's not easy, but we *can* learn to suspend our beliefs in order to listen with a clear and open mind. If we do, we won't be one of those people referred to when people use the cliché, "You can't teach an old dog new tricks."

 Where is your cup too full? In what instances do you close yourself off because you "already know that?" It's easy to finish someone's thoughts in your head when they are speaking. But in doing so, you may very well miss what they have to offer because of the filters you've created.

Watch yourself over the next week and look for times when your cup is too full to learn something new. It may surprise you.

"Never mistake knowledge for wisdom. One helps you make a living; the other helps you make a life."

—Sandra Carey

"There is a difference between happiness and wisdom: he that thinks himself the happiest man is really so; but he that thinks himself the wisest is generally the greatest fool."

—Francis Bacon, Sr.

"We seem to gain wisdom more readily through our failures than through our successes. We always think of failure as the antithesis of success, but it isn't. Success often lies just the other side of failure."

—Leo F. Buscaglia

90. That Motivation Stuff Doesn't Work!

"We don't receive wisdom; we must discover it for ourselves after a journey that no one can take for us or spare us."

—Marcel Proust

I ran into an old acquaintance of mine awhile back and in the course of our conversation we got around to asking what each of us was doing. When I told him about SuccessNet, he said, "Oh, you're in the motivation business."

I acknowledged that motivation was part of what we did, even though that's not quite the way I would have described it.

But then he said something interesting. He said, "I've tried that stuff before—went to hear one of those motivational speakers—but it didn't last more than a day or so."

I'd heard it before from others and I still don't get it. Why would someone think that being motivated or inspired is something you should do once and never have to do again?

It reminded me of Zig Ziglar's famous line, "Motivation doesn't last, but neither does taking a bath. That's why we recommend it *daily*."

The process of getting and staying motivated is just that—a process. You are never done. Just as you feed your body every day, you need to feed your mind every day.

The problem is that most people's mental diet is negative. It serves to de-motivate rather than motivate. Certainly one seminar or limited exposure to good information cannot be expected to overcome a lifetime of mental malnutrition.

We must stand guard at the doorway of our minds. If we don't choose and control what goes into our mind, there's no telling *what* will get in there.

I believe this is one of the reasons why we're experiencing such rapid growth in our membership. Many people are realizing they need constant reminders and regular infusions of positive, stimulating and inspiring ideas.

To operate at our best we need support. There's no need to try and go it alone. Anyone who has achieved great success did so with the help of many others. Why should we be any different?

The truth is, no one can really motivate us. Nor can we truly motivate others. All we can do is plant seeds and shape the environment that's most conducive to growth and vigor.

We're either self-motivated or self-defeated. But by taking control over what we read, listen to, see and experience, we position ourselves for success. We are motivated to do the things we need to do in order to achieve what we desire.

It's been said that our lives will be the same in five years as it is today except for the books we read, the people we meet and the tapes we listen to.

By maintaining our exposure to the good, the clean, the powerful, the inspiring and the uplifting, we're nourishing our minds and positively affecting our attitudes. It's all about what we think about. And by creating the right environment and feeding our minds healthy things, our thinking will be the kind of thinking that keeps us motivated and inspired.

That "motivational stuff" may not last, but it *does* work.

 What are the support systems you've put in place—or *could* put in place—to help you stay motivated? What are the actions you take regularly to help you operate at your best?

"Ability is what you're capable of doing. Motivation determines what you do. Attitude determines how well you do it."

—Lou Holtz

"Motivation is what gets you started. Habit is what keeps you going."

—Jim Rohn

"Wanting something is not enough. You must hunger for it. Your motivation must be absolutely compelling in order to overcome the obstacles that will invariably come your way."

—Les Brown

91. Let's Clean This Place Up!

"The world is not to be put in order; the world is order incarnate. It is for us to put ourselves in unison with this order."

—Henry Miller

A few years ago, I was the publisher of a magazine called *Creating Excellence*. We were nearing an important advertising deadline and were a long way from reaching our sales objectives.

I called a full staff meeting for some green-light thinking on ways we could bring in new business and fill the holes we had in the upcoming issue.

There were several good ideas tossed about with almost everyone contributing—except for Ann. Ann always had something helpful to offer, so it was out of character that she hadn't said anything.

When there was a lull in the brainstorming, she got everybody's attention when she said, "Let's clean this place up!"

Everyone turned to her with puzzlement and asked her to explain. She suggested that we devote an entire day to clean the office from top to bottom.

Now, a magazine production space is a busy place and not always one that appears neat and organized. Ours definitely fit this description. It had been a long while since it had been completely cleaned.

Her suggestion wasn't met with immediate enthusiasm, but in keeping with our rule of not disparaging any ideas brought up in a brainstorming session, Ann was allowed to outline why she thought it was more than just a good idea.

In spite of the fact we were already behind in our work, she maintained that taking a day to put our "home" in order would enable us to work and sell from a better place.

She added another dimension to something I had said many times about successful sales, "It's not so much what you say, but the space you say it *from*." She convinced us that it was indeed worth it to create a new place to work from—one that provided a new perspective.

The cleanup went beyond the Friday we scheduled and into the weekend. Some even came in to paint. With everyone helping, the entire office looked and *felt* different.

And so did we.

It worked! We all pulled together to hit our sales goal. Everyone felt the change in attitude. We had more pride, and we felt more organized. We also sold more ads. Our customers could sense it.

We embodied excellence, which was what we were selling.

 Take a good look at your workspace. Is it inspiring? Is it enjoyable to spend time there? If not, have at it. Make it some-thing to be proud of. You'll find yourself being more productive and experience more joy in doing so.

"Life is denied by lack of attention, whether it be to cleaning windows or trying to write a masterpiece."

—Nadia Boulanger

"There should be less talk; a preaching point is not a meeting point. What do you do then? Take a broom and clean someone's house. That says enough."

—Mother Teresa

92. Humor Can Save Your Life

*"You are only young once, and if you work it right,
once is enough."*

—Joe E. Lewis

The story goes that a certain court jester went too far one day and insulted his king. The king became so infuriated he sentenced the jester to be executed. His court pleaded with the king to have mercy for this man who had served him well for so many years. After a time, the king relented only enough to give the jester his *choice* as to how he would like to die.

True to form, the jester replied, "If it's all the same to you, my Lord, I'd like to die of old age."

Certainly in this case, a good sense of humor saved the man's life. It's true for us as well. We may not be faced with a situation where our wit will save us from an execution, but our sense of humor and the ability to laugh at things has proven health benefits that extend and improve our quality of life.

Norman Cousins, in his book *Anatomy of an Illness*, wrote about how he recovered from a life-threatening and incurable condition. He rented films of comedies and watched them for hours on end in his hospital room. He had nothing to lose since he'd been diagnosed as terminal.

His "experiment" turned out to be a classic example of the healing powers of laughter. He lived years longer than doctors more than once had predicted.

If it worked for Cousins with a life-threatening illness, it can work for us to enhance and protect our good health. We should laugh often and heartily. It's good for our digestion and our disposition.

Besides, life's too important to take seriously.

———❦———

"A person without a sense of humor is like a wagon without springs, jolted by every pebble in the road."

—Henry Ward Beecher

93. Escape vs. Renewal

I'm just back from a cruise in the Caribbean. It was our first Success Retreat with members and guests coming from one end of the continent to the other. The weather was perfect, the food was great and the company was inspiring. We had three presenters other than myself. Each of them shared from their hearts and minds their particular points of wisdom about their journey of success.

Among other things, Phil Humbert talked about getting rich slowly— consistently building wealth rather than going for the big, high-risk wins. Diana Nightingale told us how she met the great Earl Nightingale and the seven years they spent together before his passing in 1989. Tim Cook shared how his career with Dale Carnegie has been driven by what "feels right" and how well it's worked for him. I spoke on the principle and power of attraction—how it's easier (and less tiring) to attract than pursue.

I can think of nothing better than spending a week with people who care about things that matter, who want to make a difference. Everyone had a great time. For me it was a good balance between relaxation, stimulating conversation, sharing ideas, playing and exploring new destinations.

One of the things that struck me on this trip was the contrast between our group and the hundreds of others on the ship. It definitely was a carnival atmosphere aboard as people of all ages, including college kids on spring break, partied their way from Miami to Grand Cayman to Montego Bay, Jamaica and back to Florida. To me, it looked like many of them were working hard at having fun. They were escaping their world and their life for a few days, and they wanted to make the most of it.

For most of our group, this wasn't the case. Don't get me wrong—we were having fun—we were enjoying the break from our everyday lives. But we love what we do, and I think we vacationed from a different place than so many of the others. When you're following your purpose and living the life you want, you vacation for renewal rather than escape.

And when you do what you love, it doesn't feel like work. The need for escaping it goes away. It's still good to take a break, but it feels different. And it is.

Our objective for our first SuccessNet Retreat was to experience renewal rather than escape. I think we were quite successful.

94. How Much Do You Weigh in *Emotional* Pounds?

"We are injured and hurt emotionally, not so much by other people or what they say and don't say, but by our own attitude and our own response."

—Maxwell Maltz

In spite of the fact that half of North Americans are overweight and that losing weight is often the number one thing we can do to improve our health, our energy and our longevity, this article is not about physical pounds.

What I talk about here is weight of another kind—emotional weight. You might be tempted to say that you don't have any emotional baggage. Perhaps you consider yourself emotionally fit. And you may be right.

I recently experienced my wife—one of the most emotionally healthy people I know—become lighter before my eyes as she expressed something she had long hidden. It wasn't a big thing. It was just something she had been too polite about—a feeling she didn't want to share for fear of hurting someone. When she did, she felt a weight removed. She felt and *looked* lighter.

The word emotion is from the Latin, exmovēre—to move. So it literally means energy in motion. Unfortunately, our culture and our beliefs often cause us to stop the flow of our emotions. Our feelings are blocked in our bodies and this inhibits us from being our best. When this happens, our feelings are no longer in motion—they're dead weight. This saps our energy and spoils our clarity.

Certainly there are times when particular emotions are inappropriate to display. The ability to master our emotions is often a measure of maturity and one of the things that makes us a civilized society. But if we constantly stuff our feelings and don't express them, they become, at best, unnecessary baggage—extra weight dragging us down. At worst, they become bottled up energy that can explode in catastrophic ways.

Men especially have a hard time expressing their emotions. They often fear a display of emotion will look like weakness. This just isn't true. By expressing how we truly feel and releasing the pent-up feelings, we free ourselves to be more of who we truly are—we become more powerful.

And it's a learned skill. We get better at it the more we do it—especially when we take responsibility for those feelings instead of blaming something or somebody else for them. This is where we truly become empowered.

The information age in which we live often disparages our emotions. Bertrand Russell wrote, "We know too much and feel too little. At least we feel too little of those creative emotions from which a good life spring." Many scientists believe that humans are the only species on the planet who have emotions. And yet, our intellect often discounts and discourages this important part of our humanity.

We all need a safe place to express our feelings—the ones that feel good and the ones that don't: an understanding loved one, trusted friends or even a professional. The important thing is to do it—and do it regularly. In doing so, we allow ourselves to experience more of our power, to see things more clearly (not filtered through blocked emotions) and to be more present.

 I encourage you to get in touch with those feelings (usually the not-so-pleasant ones) which you have left unexpressed. Trust me, you have them. It's not easy at first. But if you do, you'll feel and look lighter.

"People often say that this or that person has not yet found himself. But the self is not something one finds, it is something one creates."

—Thomas Szasz

95. What's Holding You Back?

Oftentimes we've set a goal, but don't seem to make much progress toward its achievement. When faced with an unrealized goal, it's easy to beat ourselves up for not making it happen.

If you're not making the progress you'd like to be enjoying, there are several questions you can ask yourself in order to get to the heart of the matter.

What am I Afraid of?

I'd been working on a book for over a year. Most of it was done. I just seemed to find all kinds of other things to do instead of getting it ready for publishing. I began to wonder why I wasn't going for it.

What came up was that I was afraid of having it published and not selling enough copies. As long as it never came out, I never had to deal with its possible failure.

This might seem obvious to you, but it wasn't to me. I just thought I was procrastinating. I was, but the reason was at an almost unconscious level. By finding what was behind the procrastination, I was able to see what I needed to do.

Is it Really *My* Goal?

Sometimes we set goals because we think we should. Or we let other people set goals for us. When we don't take the necessary action to accomplish our objective, it could be it's because the goal is not truly ours. Any important goal requiring our best efforts must be ours and ours alone.

Is it Worthwhile?

Sometimes we set goals on a whim. Maybe you got excited about something and wrote down a goal. But later, it became just another item on the list of things to do. You've lost sight of the value this goal will bring to you.

If this is the case, begin to look at the payoffs in relation to what it's going to cost you in time, energy and resources to achieve it. Sometimes a goal just isn't worth it.

And remember, it's not about the goal. What's really important is what you become in the pursuit of the goal.

96. Your Distinctive Mark

"The great and glorious masterpiece of man
is how to live with purpose."

—Michel Eyquem de Montaigne

My grandmother was always fascinated by the fact that with all the billions of people who have lived, there have never been two people exactly alike. When you think about it, it *is* a bit mind-boggling.

There are nearly 6 billion people on the planet. And never before have so many had such easy access to what's going on around the globe. With all these people and all this knowledge of what others are doing, it's easy to feel inconsequential.

We sometimes compare ourselves to others and wonder what unique talent we have to offer. What difference can we make? What's our special place in the world?

The truth is we're all unique. We each have something special to contribute. The challenge is in discovering what that is. I consider it our sacred duty to discover and demonstrate our unique potential. And I think we're unfulfilled unless we're doing so.

It is to this issue that Sir Cecil Beaton was speaking when he wrote, "Be daring, be different, be impractical, be anything that will assert integrity of purpose and imaginative vision against the play-it-safers, the creatures of the commonplace, the slaves of the ordinary."

And yet, it appears that few people spend much time thinking about what their purpose is, what they really want, what they have to offer and preparing how to best deliver that to the world. Most people spend more time planning a family vacation than they do planning their lives.

 How can you leave your unique mark of distinction upon the world? Think about it. Ponder it. Open yourself to the belief that you and you alone have a special purpose—because you do.

And when your days are done, you can say you truly lived—that you have made a difference.

97. Living Full Out, 100%, No Matter What

"Every man dies; not every man really lives."

—William Wallace, Braveheart

The movie Braveheart, starring and directed by Mel Gibson, is one of my favorites.

It's the story of the legendary William Wallace in his valiant struggle to free Scotland from the oppressive King Longshanks of England. It's a bloody and violent film (although not gratuitously so) filled with treachery, injustice, betrayal and courage.

For me, one of the most profound lines in the entire movie was uttered by Sir Wallace shortly before he was tortured and executed by his enemies. The princess of Wales was pleading for his life and begging Wallace to swear allegiance to the King, thereby avoiding a slow and excruciatingly painful death. She says to Wallace, "If you do not, you will surely die." To which Wallace responds, "Every man dies; not every man really lives."

It was as true in the 1300s as it is today. We will all surely die. The only question is when and where. If we have the chance to reflect upon our life before we pass, will we say that we truly lived?

Most people in the twilight of their lives have more regrets for what they *didn't* do than for what they did. They wish they had done more, seen more and felt more. They wish they had lived with more gusto.

Don't let that happen to you. Life is not something to be endured. Life is meant to be lived full out. But most of us, for a variety of reasons, have pulled back—we live carefully and guarded—not allowing the full expression of who we are and what we believe.

Be enthusiastic! It's contagious. John Wesley said, "Set yourself on fire and people will come for miles to watch you burn." You don't have to be flamboyant about it either (although it might help). Genuine enthusiasm lies just beneath the surface and is always bubbling to the top. What many people think of as enthusiasm is simply exuberance pasted on the outside.

It's always been amazing to me that people will demonstrate more enthusiasm and excitement for their favorite sports team than they do for their own life. They think nothing of acting a little—or a lot—crazy rooting for their team but have little or no enthusiasm for the *big* game—their life.

Forget about what people might think. Like Mel Brooks said, "If you're alive, you've got to flap your arms and legs, you got to jump around a lot, you've got to make a lot of noise, because life is the very opposite of death . . . You've got to be noisy, or at least your thoughts should be noisy and colorful and lively."

That way, when your turn on the planet is done, you (and others) can say you lived your life, you *really* lived.

 I invite you—no, I implore you—to look carefully at how you're living your own life. Where are you just going through the motions? Where are you not living full out? What would your life be like if you gave your all—to your job, your family, your community, your beliefs, to your mate?

Living full out is the only way to really live.

"There is no chance, no destiny, no fate, that can circumvent or hinder or control the firm resolve of a determined soul."

—Ella Wheller Wilcox

"Brave men are all vertebrates; they have their softness on the surface and their toughness in the middle."

—G. K. Chesterton

98. Your Success is an Inside Job

"An investment in yourself will pay dividends for the rest of your life. It won't depreciate, it will appreciate. It will never be devalued or stolen. Clearly, your inner portfolio is the best investment you can make."

We spend a good deal of time and money on the outside of our bodies. We pay for haircuts and styles, we buy cosmetics, lotions and colognes. We purchase expensive clothes. We spend many minutes each day primping, combing, washing, feeding and, hopefully, exercising our bodies. Most of this activity is devoted to adorning or nurturing the outside of our bodies.

But what about the inside? Doesn't it make sense to spend as much money and effort caring for our emotional, spiritual and mental side as we do on our exteriors? You might find it easy to agree with this notion, but I'll bet you'd be hard-pressed to find many people who spend as much on inner work as outer work.

With the exception of a formal education, most people have no budget for the inside job of success.

What about you? What investment have you made in your attitude? How are you improving it? What new skills and knowledge have you acquired? What do you do to insure fresh, stimulating ideas for yourself and your company? What are you doing on a daily basis to be your best?

Everything you do to improve yourself will last the rest of your life. How many material acquisitions will last that long? Think of personal development not as putting something on top of what you are, but rather developing more of who you already are. Like the development of a picture from its negative, real self-development just exposes more of what already lies hidden.

 Take a hard look at exactly what you're doing and what you're spending on developing your mental, spiritual and emotional stock. Are you reading books that feed your mind? Are you listening to tapes that educate, inspire and stimulate you? What are you doing to enhance your emotional well-being?

It doesn't matter where you begin as long as you start. Pick an area you'd like to improve upon and have at it. It can be fun as well as rewarding.

99. Good Judgment vs. Being Judgmental

Developing good judgment is worthy of our best efforts. Being able to consistently make informed and considered decisions enables us to achieve the results we desire.

But being judgmental isn't the same thing. Being judgmental is not about discernment. It's about judging the beliefs, actions, inactions and opinions of others.

Here's what I see as the difference between judging people and having an opinion: an opinion is a viewpoint, a judgment based upon observation in the context of our own experience and bias. We all have them, and we're entitled to them.

However, when we have an opinion with a "charge" to it, when our opinion is fueled with emotion—like anger and agitation—then the opinion is most likely a judgment. We're making someone wrong. We're being judgmental.

It's a waste of time and energy to be so invested in another person's actions or beliefs. It's challenging enough to change ourselves, and it's virtually impossible to change other people. It's far more productive to invest in improving ourselves.

Certainly, there are times when someone else's actions or inactions negatively impact us. And in these instances, it's incumbent upon us to make our requests known. In doing so, we may be able to influence a person to change. But making demands instead of requests rarely works.

Most of the time, being judgmental is about being right. And the "right" or "wrong" in any given situation is rarely factual.

 Check yourself when you're in a debate or in disagreement with someone. Are you in reaction rather than just stating your case? Are you trying to be "right" and invested in them agreeing with you?

If so, you're being judgmental. And this kind of judging is toxic to you and your relationship with that person.

Notice the times when you're stepping over the boundary of speaking your truth and judging another.

And be sure you don't judge *yourself*. Just recognize what you did or are doing, and resolve to do better next time. *That's* good judgment.

100. Turning Ideas into Income

In the early days of SuccessNet, I found myself in need of a new computer. The one I was using was just too slow, and I needed to upgrade.

During one of my meetings with my friend, Joe Donnelly, I told him what I wanted. I also said I didn't want to pay for it out of cash flow or go into debt. I was looking for a way to trade services.

To his credit, Joe took this concept one step further. He suggested that instead of trading services, which would use up my most precious resource (time) I should look to trade something I already had—something that wouldn't use up my inventory of time.

We started brainstorming about what this could be. We approached it by asking the question, "What do my clients need that I might provide?" We focused on increasing their sales. We talked about my clients and zeroed in on one that sold computers.

We kicked around a good number of general ideas, and I left the meeting with my head spinning about several concepts I might present to my client.

I mapped out a plan of action and requested a meeting with the computer client. In that meeting, I told them that I had an idea and wanted to sell it to them. I asked that they compensate me with a new computer if they used the idea. If they didn't think it was worthwhile, they would owe me nothing. They agreed.

I then outlined my idea for increasing their sales, what the sales increase was likely to be and how to go about implementing the program.

They bought it. It took a little time to put the whole deal together, but the overall time investment was minimal. I sold an idea, and I got a new computer and a 17" monitor.

The fact is, I've been selling ideas all my life. But I usually had to make the ideas work in order to gain any value from them. This was the first time I could remember actually getting paid for a raw idea. Instead of selling—or trading—my time, I was selling my idea. And it was fun.

 Look for creative and lateral ways to accomplish your goals. Oftentimes, we lock ourselves into a certain way to achieve what we want, and in the process, we overlook some innovative ways to get where we want to go.

What can you trade for something you want? Start brainstorming today to solve your problems and achieve your goals. You can do it.

 Be sure to take a look at our new "Idea to Income" Audio Seminar. In it, Sarah Pond outlines how to conceive, nurture, cultivate and harvest ideas—and turn them into cash.

www.SuccessNet.org/idea2income.htm

"Innovation is the specific instrument of entrepreneurship. The act that endows resources with a new capacity to create wealth."

—Peter F. Drucker

"A pile of rocks ceases to be a rock when somebody contemplates it with the idea of a cathedral in mind."

—Antoine de Saint-Exupery

"Everything begins with an idea."

—Earl Nightingale

101. You Bet it's Personal—it's Business!

Recently, I heard the president of a company say, "It's not personal, it's just business." The phrase had about the same warmth and comfort as when it was uttered in "The Godfather"—right after someone was killed.

Business is all about relationships and relationships *are* personal. To dismiss the importance of personal relationships with the excuse that it's "just business" is usually a cop-out. It's old-school and it lacks integrity.

Of course, there are times when we have to make difficult business decisions which adversely affect people. But we're far better off to acknowledge that it's personal.

A World Class Business demands close working relationships. They don't have to be super-intimate, but they do have to be honest and open.

Some people are reluctant to have close relationships with subordinates or supervisors in order to avoid uncomfortable and/or painful situations. But I think a world class company is one that makes the tough decisions fully cognizant of how business decisions affect people. It's *all* personal.

When I heard that CEO say "It's not personal, it's just business," it was a good indicator of how little she valued good relationships. She may have believed she could separate business from friendship, but I don't think most people can—or should.

A company's bottom line is determined by its *front* line. People are the most valuable assets, and good stewardship requires that we treat every single person as just that—a *person*. They're not a commodity, regardless of the fact that many companies treat them as such.

Yes, it *is* personal—it's business. And in my opinion, it should be.

Commit to developing and nurturing good relationships with everyone in your company. Take a genuine interest in them, and you'll find them doing likewise. Enemies never help you—friends do. Don't let your judgments of anyone stand in the way of your own or your organization's success.

And remember, people don't care how much you know unless they know how much you care.

Resources

Books

- ☐ ***Success: A Spiritual Matter***
  www.SuccessNet.org/spirit/

- ☐ ***101 Best Ways to Get Ahead***
  Solid gold advice from the world's most successful people
  www.101BestWays.com

- ☐ ***101 Best Ways to Simplify Your Life*** (late 2005)
  www.101BestWays.com

- ☐ ***101 Best Ways to Stay Motivated and Inspired*** (early 2006)
  www.101BestWays.com

Reports

- ☐ ***101 Things I've Learned in My 50 Trips Around the Sun*** (free)
  www.SuccessNet.org/reports.htm

- ☐ ***101 Ways to Save Time and Be More Effective***
  www.SuccessNet.org/101savetime.htm

- ☐ ***How to Form Your Own Success Team***
  www.SuccessNet.org/teams.htm

- ☐ ***How to Write a Mission Statement***
  Creating Vision and Mission Statements That Work!
  www.SuccessNet.org/mission-report.htm

- ☐ ***10 Essential Keys to Personal Effectiveness*** (free)
  www.SuccessNet.org/subscribes.htm

- ☐ ***101 Best Tools & Resources to Run Your Internet Business***
  The top must-have tools and resources Infopreneurs
  use to get more done with less hassle.
  www.SuccessNet.org/101bestways/resources

- ☐ ***101 Ways to Save Time & Be More Effective***
  How to get more done in less time.
  www.SuccessNet.org/101savetime.htm

Tools

- ☐ ***Laser Questions*™**
  Get clear, get focused, get ahead.
  www.SuccessNet.org/laserq.htm

☐ *Priorities*™
Determine your most important, biggest pay-off, mission-aligned goals, purchases, challenges and objectives.
www.SuccessNet.org/priorities.htm

Programs, Courses & Other Resources

☐ **SuccessNet Gold Membership**
Discounts, private web site access, insider information and much more.
www.SuccessNet.org/join.htm

☐ **Freedom to Achieve™ System**
www.SuccessNet.org/fta

☐ **Inspirational and Motivational Quotation Library (free)**
www.SuccessNet.org/library.htm

☐ **World Class Business™**
Take your business to the next level.
www.WorldClassBusiness.com

☐ **Your Core Values™ eCourse**
Discover, define and begin living in accordance with your true values.
www.YourCoreValues.com

☐ **Creating Excellence™ (coming late 2005)**
Daily motivation and inspiration to help you excel. For employers and employees who want to make every day more productive and fulfilling.
www.CreatingExcellence.com

☐ **Step Up to Success™ Course**
Learn the fundamental principles of success.
www.SuccessNet.org/stepup.htm

☐ **SuccessMark™ Cards**
Inspirational and motivational online greeting cards (free)
www.SuccessMarkCards.com

☐ **Michael Angier, speaker, coach and consultant**
Michael works with senior executives who want to build world-class companies and with people who want to do value-driven work.
www.MichaelAngier.com

Index

The SuccessNet Creed

The principles and beliefs upon which SuccessNet was founded and the guidelines by which it operates.

WE BELIEVE we have a responsibility—a sacred trust—to conduct business with the utmost integrity and with impeccable ethics. We further believe that this responsibility goes beyond mere legality and encompasses a sense of fair play for all involved. We play win-win and we play it well.

WE BELIEVE that a balanced life is the only life worth living. Without it, no real fulfillment can be experienced. Having financial success at the expense of one's health or one's family is not true success. We recognize that striking this balance is not easy.

WE BELIEVE success is indeed a journey and not a destination—that it's not what we achieve, but rather what we *become* in the process of our achievements. It's not what happens *to* us but what we do about what happens to us that makes the difference.

WE BELIEVE we must give in order to receive—that if we help enough other people get what they want, we can get what we want. We commit to serving and supporting others—to helping them realize their potential and, in the process, realize our own.

WE BELIEVE in dreams—that all great achievements in history came from the pursuit of a dream, and that it's incumbent upon us to discover, honor and fulfill the dreams we have within us.

WE BELIEVE that clarity leads to power. When we're clear on our objectives, know what our core values are and consistently focus on the things that matter, we really can accomplish anything we choose.

WE BELIEVE in the resilience and potential of the human spirit, that men and women are created in the image of God and that we're capable of accomplishing anything—although not necessarily *everything*— we set out to do.

WE BELIEVE business is all about relationships with people—that good business is built by creating relationships of trust, by keeping agreements and maintaining integrity.

WE BELIEVE that commerce has been and will continue to be a primary influence in world issues and that world peace is furthered by strong and interrelated business alliances. As business and people become more interdependent upon one another, we become freer and decrease the likelihood of armed conflict because we recognize it's impossible to sink half the ship.

WE BELIEVE that by providing excellent products and services, people will reward us with their business. When we promise a lot and deliver even more, we secure the loyalty and patronage of the consumer. We commit to constant and never-ending improvement of what we offer our customers.

WE BELIEVE the path of mastery is through the joy of creating excellence in all that we do and the way in which we do it. When we do what we love, we're not only happier, we produce better products and services.

WE BELIEVE every customer, employee, stockholder, servant, competitor and partner is first and foremost a person—a unique expression of Universal Spirit—someone who deserves our respect and consideration.

WE BELIEVE that change is not only inevitable but good; not only unpredictable, but also stimulating and educational. It's rarely comfortable, but it's essential to our growth and development. Accepting change and adapting to it will always win out over resistance.

WE BELIEVE mistakes and failures are an integral and necessary part of success and embrace them as learning experiences.

WE BELIEVE the use of knowledge is power and we are committed to our own ongoing educational process. We further believe that our knowledge is to always be used for good—never to cause harm.

WE BELIEVE that information, information technologies and the sharing of same creates more freedom. It levels the playing field, thereby reducing injustice and making it more difficult for tyranny, prejudice, misunderstanding and inequality to reign.

To order additional copies of this book and/or other 101 Best Ways books and booklets, go to www.101BestWays.com.

About SuccessNet

SuccessNet is an international association of people committed to operating at their best—to creating excellence in every aspect of their lives and throughout their respective organizations. We support people in developing the skills, knowledge, belief and passion to achieve their dreams.

> **OUR MISSION:**
> *to inform, inspire and empower people to be their best—personally and professionally.*

SuccessNet is dedicated to helping you become more knowledgeable, prosperous and effective. In addition to our publications, we provide a complete membership package dedicated to making your road to success easier and more fun.

Since 1995, over 150,000 people from all around the globe have benefited from the SuccessNet experience.

People from all walks of life become members—small-business owners, managers and people who want to get ahead in their careers. Anyone who wants to maximize their potential, improve the quality of their lives and make a lasting difference in the world.

SuccessNet is for great people who want to become even better.

Get a free subscription with your free report, *10 Essential Keys to Personal Effectiveness.*

Subscribe at www.SuccessNet.org/subscribes.htm or by sending an email to subscribe@SuccessNet.org

Visit our web site at www.SuccessNet.org

Success Networks International
Win-Win Way, PO Box 2048
So Burlington, Vermont 05407-2048 USA
Phone: 802.862.0812
Fax: 425.988.7300

About the Author

Michael Angier is the founder and CIO (Chief Inspiration Officer) of SuccessNet, the popular web-based community dedicated to helping people operate at their personal and professional best.

Michael is a father, husband, mentor, author, speaker, entrepreneur, coach and student. He's also the creator of The World Class Business™ Conference and has taught seminars and conducted workshops on goal setting, motivation and personal development in four countries.

Michael's passion is human potential. Helping people discover, develop and fulfill their dreams is his purpose, which is clearly reflected in SuccessNet. Michael is one of those individuals who has found his purpose in life and aligns all his endeavors with it.

Intrigued by the science of individual achievement early in his life, Michael has devoted himself to advancing his experience and expertise in personal and professional development for more than 30 years.

In his youth, already an ardent student of the principles of success, Michael began reading biographies of successful individuals and was fascinated by their lives and the contributions they made to the world.

Michael is married to Dawn Angier—his partner, best friend, mentor, teacher, student and confidant. They live in South Burlington, Vermont and have six children ranging in age from 13 to 33. Michael enjoys sailing, tennis, traveling, reading and helping people realize their dreams.